Fundamentals of Life

Other Book by The Author

Coffee Table Philosophy
A Book of Photos and Thoughts
First edition © 2011
Second edition © 2020
ISBN: 978-0-9856781-1-1

Fundamentals of Life

Know Yourself, Be Yourself

Rick Sorenson

Fundamentals of Life

Copyright © 2021 by Rick Sorenson

Editing by Deb Harman

The copying or distribution of the information or diagrams contained in this book without permission is a theft of the author's property. If you would like to request permission, please send a request to info@ricksorenson.com.

25 definitions contained herein are used with permission from https://www.merriam-webster.com/dictionary/ , © 2020 by Merriam-Webster, Incorporated.
5 definitions contained herein are used with permission from https://learnersdictionary.com/.
2 definitions contained herein are used with permission from https://www.wordcentral.com.

ISBN: 978-0-9856781-2-8

Acknowledgment

I want to offer a heartfelt thank you to Deb Harman whose time and dedication to editing this book made it a better book. I have learned a lot from her.

Thank you Deb.

Table of Contents

PREFACE	ix
INTRODUCTION	xiii

Part 1: The Fundamentals

BREAKING DOWN THE FUNDAMENTALS	3
LOVE	11
HONOR	29
BELIEVING	39
HOPE	49
SUMMARY OF FUNDAMENTALS	57

Part 2: Life's Realities

IMPLEMENTATION AND LIFE'S REALITIES	81
EVERYTHING IS RELATIVE	85
LEARNING	91
COMMUNICATION	99
PERCEPTION VS. FACTS	103
KNOWLEDGE	109
WISDOM	113
PRINCIPLES	115
INTEGRITY	121
TRUST	125
RESPECT	131
FRIENDSHIP	137
SELF-PRESERVATION	141
SUCCESS	145
CONTROL	149
EXPECTATIONS	155
EQUALITY	159
GREED	165

ACCOUNTABILITY & RESPONSIBILITY	167
APPROVAL & ACCEPTANCE	171
WORRY & FEAR	175
PAIN	183
HATE	187
DEATH	191
PRIORITIES	195
THE SELF-THINGS	199
MAKING DECISIONS	205
REACTIONARY TRIGGERS	209
THE PURPOSE OF LIFE	215
SUMMARY THUS FAR	219

Part 3: Coffee Table

COFFEE TABLE INTRODUCTION	227
COFFEE TABLE EXPANSION	233
COFFEE TABLE WRAP-UP	281
FUNDAMENTALS OF LIFE WRAP-UP	285
EPILOGUE	A-i
BIBLIOGRAPHY	A-iii
Index	A-ix

PREFACE

A Little About the Author

Why This Book Now?

This book has been in the works for most of my life. I now find myself to be defined by others, and probably general society, as elderly; although being in my sixties at this point certainly does not *seem* elderly. I can, however, remember a time when I thought that forty was elderly. Everything is relative.

I've long had the desire and even the need to share something with others. I had been so frustrated with my most recent corporate position and I was looking forward to retirement when I could do the things that I want to do, all of which involve creating something. Creating in the form of writing books, writing music, photography and whatever else comes to mind. All of these admittedly leave something behind and hopefully bring something of value to others. I have a need to do that; it has been with me for as long as I can remember but it became more pronounced when I had my first cancer, which is now more than forty years ago. This need had been somewhat put on a bit of a backburner and in the last few years has come more to the forefront with some feeling of urgency.

I don't want to run out of time. I don't want to spend so much time on a job that provides little benefit to anyone and even less satisfaction to me. What that job provided was money and that just felt more and more selfish. I tried to make the work more beneficial to others and more satisfying to me but that was met with resistance at almost every step. The passing of Prince, for some reason, had something to do with the feeling that there is little time left as yet another creative person that still had more to give is now gone. However, the event that hit me the hardest was the passing of my sister. I had lost my father, my mother, a brother and another sister but losing Judy hit me by far the hardest. In many ways, she was certainly the closest sibling that I had and her passing was way too early and unexpected but it was not as early as my other sister and no earlier than my brother. The realization that hits me hard is that, from that family perspective, I am alone. I am the only one left. There is no one left that has those shared family memories. No one. No one to say "Remember when…?". I look at a family picture and I am the only one left. The other fact that is undoubtedly a factor in my feelings is that all three of my siblings and my dad did not make it past seventy. Three of the four made it to seventy and my oldest sister only to her forties. I am now in my mid-sixties. Do I have less than five years left? How much less? That isn't much time to create the things that I would like to leave for others.

I am sure that many people have similar feelings about "the end" but I have no idea if many others feel the obligation that I feel. I don't think that my feelings are egotistical, as I don't feel a sense of superiority but rather a *need* to share what I have. I believe that I can make things better for others. I actually believe that everybody can in their own way if they choose to do so. I believe that I might be able to offer an insight that may impact the lives of others. That is why I am writing again. I know that I want to write music and create more artwork but the sense that I have something to share is very pronounced right now in writing. I feel that if I die before getting it out, something would die with me. That would have been my fault for not getting to it and I would have wasted time and part of my life. Life is way too short and I know that is a cliché but IT IS.

It was difficult to retire for a few reasons but the need to move on was strong. I had to walk away even though my employer made me a very lucrative offer to stay a little longer. Despite some thinking I was crazy for leaving, I was very comfortable with my decision. I knew that I needed to do other things (this book for one) and time is limited. I knew in my heart that other things were more important. I just came from the doctor today, three weeks after retiring and they suspect that I have lung cancer that has metastasized. There is more testing to be done and it has just begun. The diagnosis was not really a surprise to me and it doesn't change my purpose; it just emphasizes that fact that I need to work every day to create as much as possible. I believe, other than the love that I have for friends and family, it is the most I have to offer.

I do not write about these events in my life to share my history or to make it sound like I have had some difficult times. All of these events, decisions, and traumas are personal to me and why would you care? I share them as evidence that life events can be, and hopefully are, used as triggers to better understanding and self-awareness. It is unfortunate that so many people need this type of life jolt to address who they are and how they feel about life. People can find this over time but these types of events create reminders that we don't have forever and there is a need to prioritize. The idea that life's traumas have an impact on heightening our awareness of priorities is addressed multiple times throughout this book.

The conclusions that I have made, the actions that I have taken, and the thought process leading to them has been driven by who I am; my fundamentals. These life events did not create my fundamentals, they just enabled me to see them more clearly.

Rick Jaeson

INTRODUCTION

I realize that these words and thoughts are created by me entering my "later" years. Age certainly changes our thoughts and perspective and hopefully all of us continue to grow throughout our lives (refer to the Learning chapter of this book for more information on how people learn). It is a fact however, that my four core fundamentals have been with me from a very young age. I just did not have a label for them and hadn't actually understood what they were. My actions as a teenager and my thesis in college substantiate that these fundamentals have been with me for a long time. The ability to associate them with other aspects of life and articulate them into this writing has certainly grown over time.

This brings me to this writing and what better place to start than with the fundamentals. The things that I see and feel others would benefit from mostly seem to be fundamentals. My only hope is that if they are fundamentals and so basic, that they can be presented in a more enlightening or thought-provoking way, otherwise this writing is for naught.

I am concerned that what I need to write will come out as a bunch of clichés because as you get older, those clichés take on more and more meaning. I speak of getting older as though I know how everyone else feels about it and it is easy for people to assume that what they feel is what others feel. This is evident in the words and actions of other people. A very simple example of that are the words that people use that can have so many different meanings and people give no thought to the way others may understand those words because we speak from the context that we know. Right now, a cliché evident to me is "Walk a mile in their shoes."

The fact that a cliché pops into my head not only confirms my fear that this book could turn into a bunch of clichés but brings to mind that rather than fight it, maybe they can be used to make a point. Clichés are phrases that come to be what they are because they are over simplified, overused and generally obvious statements of thoughts or situations (maybe even truisms) that most people can or should relate to. Why not occasionally use clichés and hopefully add more depth to them? There are some clichés that could be and maybe have been a book unto themselves. Whether they come out as clichés or not, it is time to get on with this book.

I do not have false expectations that the growth that happens with maturity and your own life events can be circumvented, but I truly do hope that something in this book might be able to enhance or even speed the process. This book is not just my philosophy; it is my heart and soul.

Fundamentals of Life

This book is divided into three separate sections:

1. Part 1: The Fundamentals: The explanation of fundamentals and how they are used.
2. Part 2: Life's Realities: Supporting and inhibiting realities of life.
3. Part 3: Coffee Table: Expands on the meaning and background of the photos in my first book.

PART 1
The Fundamentals

The Explanation of Fundamentals and How They Are Used

Chapter 1-1
BREAKING DOWN THE FUNDAMENTALS

The concept of fundamentals is based on philosophies, beliefs, and observations about life. Everything is both simple and complex, and that concept is explored throughout this book. The short explanation of this statement is that by looking at the simple aspect of something, a lot of "noise" can be eliminated that has no bearing on the situation. That may be the end of it or, at a minimum, the amount of complexity left to address is far less once the noise has been eliminated.

We all face decisions every day; some are big and some are small but there is no escaping the decisions. Even the choice to not make a decision is a decision. Our decisions impact our life as well as the lives of countless others. Our decisions come from a place of who we are. Who we are is certainly complex and can be very different for everyone but there are underlying *fundamentals* that define who we are and therefore are the basis of our decisions. Creating and using fundamentals is a method by which simplification can be enabled.

The potential impacts and results of implementing fundamentals are explored throughout this book. One cascading impact is as follows:

1. Enable an understanding of yourself, who you are and what is important
2. Understanding yourself allows you to:
   a. Enable the "simple" part of life
   b. Consistently be true to yourself
   c. Assess yourself and your actions for continual self-improvement
3. Consistency leads to a higher level of impact on others
4. Being true to you leads to a higher level of self-esteem and self-respect
5. Consistency and self-respect lead to inner peace

Understanding our fundamentals does not give us total control of the world around us, but discovering our fundamentals and defining who we are can provide so much value to others as well as ourselves. How do we get to the point of that understanding?

This book in itself is an evolution of learning. This book has been in the works for over four years and I came to the conclusion that fundamentals need to first be constrained. Over those four years, more and more *fundamentals* were added. The resulting volume of fundamentals made me wonder if a logical definition of a fundamental had been exceeded, and it most certainly had.

Definitions were researched, which is a common practice in this book, and none of them mentioned that there is a limit to the number of fundamentals but some definitions used fundamental as a singular. Referring to fundamental as a singular allows for an interpretation that there can be only one; which certainly cannot be a constraint. After reading various Internet definitions, I turned to Merriam-Webster and the first of three definitions of fundamental. Two others did not really apply, as they were specific to music and frequency amplitude. This one works and provides enough direction:

> **fundamental:** *(noun) "...one of the minimum constituents without which a thing or a system would not be what it is..."* [1]

The word "minimum" forced some prioritization on my crowded list of ideas for fundamentals. The impact to this book was evaluating and reducing the list into the minimal fundamentals. The rest of the ideas became operational and implementation realities of life. In some cases they are the way the fundamentals are implemented and in some cases they are the reason to utilize the fundamentals. These operating realities from the original list of ideas are primarily the *whats* and *hows*. The resulting fundamentals are the *whys*.

It may be clear by now that this use of fundamentals is not about the physical fundamentals required to live such as food, water and air. The fundamentals in this book define who we are and how we act and react. They are the "why" behind our actions. Many times our fundamentals are not a conscious answer to the question of why; they are just who we are. Understanding that further enables their reusability, enhancement, and effectiveness.

The result is a core set of fundamentals that consists of:
- Love
- Hope
- Believing
- Honor

Why these four fundamentals? Some may say these are idealistic and that this is not a realistic view of the world. That is definitely not the case. There is no expectation that everyone will have these exact fundamentals, or that because these fundamentals drive my decisions that the outcomes will be representative of the intent. There is also no expectation that anyone, including myself, is able to be perfect in adherence to his or her fundamentals. Fundamentals act as grounding points, points from which to measure and improve, and a place to define who you are. More importantly, they help you understand and more consistently be who you are. Again, being who you are brings inner peace.

My original set of *fundamental* ideas included concepts such as learning, respect, friendship, priorities and so on. Dozens of ideas were gathered over time and were believed to be fundamental. I forced myself to ask why I considered each of them to be fundamental and found that in many cases there was a reason or reasons at a lower level. It is also important to keep in mind that fundamentals are used to make decisions. Finding the lowest common denominator of fundamentals is certainly more difficult than the mathematical implementation of this concept.

Let me give you an example in finding the lowest common denominator. This example is not an example of life's fundamentals because it does not meet the criteria of the *why* and the use to make decisions. I use this example because creating categories, which is the grouping of your *ideas* for fundamentals, can itself be a challenge.

Say that over time you came to a conclusion that you were reliant on electricity because you use power tools, kitchen appliances, lights and other tools that make your life easier. Let's say you have another conclusion that you are reliant upon transportation and you land on wheels as being a category for transportation. What about planes? They have wheels in addition to wings so wheels seem to be okay; but what about electric cars? Are electric cars now in both categories (electricity and wheels)? Now consider that those other power tools and appliances do not all use electricity; some are gas powered and some are simply powered by muscle. See where I am going? Everything that I have been talking about, regardless of it being tools, appliances, or transportation is dependent on some form of power to make them work. Later, you remember that a boat is a form of transportation so that invalidates your original thought of wheels but power still applies to boats so your selection of power is still intact. This is an example of continuous improvement, validation and cross-checking that serves to make your fundamentals more stable. Power might be a confusing word to use for this since some could interpret power as something that a person strives for rather than a source of power. I would, in this case, select energy as the lowest common denominator. Even with that selection, it is important that the definition of the lowest common denominator is "tuned".

That is the focus of the next chapters regarding the four fundamentals that have been selected.

It may be that you feel you have your core fundamentals defined and maybe they are a different set of fundamentals. I certainly cannot tell you that you are wrong because only you can know who you are. It may also be that you have not thought about the concept of core fundamentals and yet be assured that you have them. They may not be top of mind, or they may not be what you would think or want them to be, but you have them. Finding them, tuning them and applying them is the point of this book. I, as with anyone else, can only offer considerations.

Creating your own fundamentals can seem like a daunting task but it should not be viewed in that regard. That does not mean that it is easy or that it will happen fast; it does mean that any task that is viewed as daunting is in jeopardy of never being done. To that end, one suggestion may be to start with the fundamentals that I have outlined and modify, tweak, or change them from there. Either way, there are just a few guidelines that make sense in the fundamental creation process:

- An effective and efficient number of fundamentals is likely between two and five. Obviously, I decided on four. The reason for this is that it is difficult for all of life's fundamentals to be summarized into one fundamental. There is no cross-check, validation or forced prioritization required between fundamentals if there is only one. Cross-checks and validations are important to the creation and continuous improvement of fundamentals. Having more than one fundamental also adds to the flexibility at the time of implementation to select a different fundamental or even more likely combine them in various ways. Too many fundamentals increases the complexity and defeats the purpose of simplification.

- There should be no conflict between the fundamentals. Some situations might require prioritization, but direct conflict would negate the meaning, value and purpose of the fundamentals that conflict. Remember, part of the value is to enable the "simple". A simple example of a conflict would be power and love since love is given and power is acquired.
- Utilize life's traumas to recognize or validate the *whys* that are important to you. If they are important in a traumatic time, they are likely the most important. Understanding that is incredibly valuable, enlightening and freeing.
- Fundamentals should be positive rather than negative. It is a fact that I have a fear of heights and that fear has driven some significant decisions in my life. However, to the point of finding the *important* parts of who you are, I cannot imagine myself saying that I wish I had avoided more situations that involved heights. Just because fear, as an example of a negative, drives decisions, it does not mean that you should use fear as a fundamental to make decisions. It is better to use the fundamentals to address the fears (negatives) than have the negatives define who you are. Fears and other "negatives" are a reality of life that will be covered in Part 2 of this book.

- Fundamentals focus on the *important* decisions that define who you are or what you want to be. This one opens a can of worms, but it is another focus point that is required for honing in on the fundamentals.

These last two guidelines deserve an explanation. I intentionally used the word *important*, which is a very subjective and relative word, because only you can define what is important to you. There are chapters later in the book that go in-depth on fear, prioritization, and decisions separately, but some of that is important to the scope of the current topic of defining fundamentals. The important decisions and actions for people tend to get emphasized during a traumatic event such as already described, but you don't have to wait for one of those to start thinking about it.

Considering everything in your life, if you had one week left to live, what would you want to or need to do? Who would you want to be with? What would you want to say that had not been said? What do you want to make sure someone knows or is taken care of? Without making the thoughts about death, maybe use the approach of how do you want to be known? What adjectives describe you? The answer to these questions and more will help tune the *important* aspects of who you are and how you will find your inner peace.

A focus point of creating and using fundamentals is to make decisions but since tens of thousands of decisions get made every day, there needs to be a direction toward which subset of decisions should be the focus. Think about the potential regrets of not being who you are and the complexity and anxiety that creates. Do you think that ten years from now you will say things like, "I wish I had bacon rather than sausage for breakfast ten years ago", or "I wish that I had listened to Pink Floyd rather than Led Zeppelin on Tuesday, 6 years, 2 months and 3 days ago at 10:42 AM". There are decisions that are just *noise* in this regard. Finding that line between *important* and *noise* can be done if you focus on who you are and what you represent, but it is a life-long exercise and realizations will happen throughout your life.

There is a reason that there are separate chapters on decisions and prioritizations. Even though the focus will be on the important decisions, *all* decisions, even the seemingly innocuous ones, have the potential to have significant impact on others.

Regardless of whether you decide to use the four fundamentals outlined in this book or create your own, please read the rest of this book first to gain a better understanding of the purpose and definitions that I have outlined.

The interaction between each of the fundamentals becomes the woven fabric of the foundation and the basis on which we can live, evolve and become "better". The way we live out life is much more driven by who we are than by what happens to us, even though it very often does not seem that way. Staying above life's challenges takes fortitude, commitment and belief in yourself and your principles. It takes the fundamentals of Love, Hope, Believing and Honor.

The following chapters will explore these fundamentals and the relationship between them.

Part 1: The Fundamentals

Chapter 1-2
LOVE

Before getting to the definition(s) of love, it might be helpful to understand how love became one of the fundamentals. It is the most obvious one to me and the rest of the fundamentals fill in what love does not fully address. My initial large set of supposed fundamentals included things such as family, friendship, giving, and humanity. When I look at the most important things in my life, my family and the people that I care about are right at the top. They are the ones that I think about the most when faced with a critical time and they are the reason that I do many things. I have also expressed my need to share with others and do what I can to help even the people that I don't know. There are other factors that impacted the selection of love as a fundamental, but it is obvious that underlying these major components of life, love is an underlying *why*. It will hopefully become clearer as we walk through the definition and tuning process.

Definition

Let's grab a cliché right away, "It's love that makes the world go round" [2]. There is no more precious and valuable gift to give and to receive. There are *so* many types of love but they all have something in common in its purest form; *a willingness to prioritize another over yourself.* This may seem like an outrageous statement to some because they may know that when they say *I love you*, at least in some circumstances, it does not mean that. Let's step back and break it down. Merriam-Webster's first definition is:

> **love:** *"...a quality or feeling of strong or constant affection for and dedication to another..."* [3]

Other definitions are based on sexual attraction and this foundational component is not referring to anything sexual. You read that correctly; it is about the *why* in the foundations of life and not about sex. It is understood that may be a disappointment to some.

It is important to understand that, for the purpose of defining usable fundamentals, you are allowed, if not encouraged, to clarify the definitions. Clarification, not complete redefinition, is likely required because the dictionary definition may be too broad to be meaningful enough to allow you to use it as a basis for decisions.

You can love anyone in any type of relationship and they all may feel completely different. They may feel different because of the term *affection* that resides in the previous Merriam-Webster's definition. Affection has implications beyond some relationships that are bound by love. Love involves some level of responsibility, not out of duty but out of dedication. You can love your spouse, your friend, your relative or your neighbor.

The word *love* is thrown around like most words today that are watered down by misuse, abuse and disregard for its meaning. It becomes a spew of oratory garbage that has little truth or significance.

Part 1: The Fundamentals

This is not just specific to love but with many words. Saying *I love you* can be a habit, it can be a motivator, or a manipulator, but the value of love is not in the words, rather, it is in the actions and decisions that are made because of it.

For a moment, let's look at actions that define love rather than the actions that are required by love. In other words, if you do *X*, you love someone vs. if you love someone you will do *X*, or if you say "I love you", you wouldn't do *X*. Setting expectations, and the subsequent judgment of meeting the expectations of love is counterproductive, but recognizing the actions that show love is real evidence and is always positive. The absence of action is not part of the formula for determining love. Love is not a burden; love is a state of your heart and soul.

Another term that is sometimes intermixed with love is passion. Passion, like love, can be used in various ways and we are not going to spend a lot of time on it now, but it is certainly different than love. Passion is not a higher level of love. Passion is an intensity of emotion and it can be both positive and negative emotions. Passion can be used in conjunction with love of all categories and also with any other action or feeling including the other fundamentals.

The counterweight to love is of course hate. Love is active and hate is typically passive unless it has gone to an active level of revenge or pure evil. We are not going to spend a lot of time on hate, evil and other negative things as part of fundamentals because although negatives are a factor, they should not be part of your consistent basis for making decisions or act as the definition of who you are. They absolutely need to be recognized and dealt with, but to spend more time on them here might risk the negatives becoming the point, when negatives are not what life should be about even though they are a real part of our world.

The Difference Between Love and a Relationship

This is an important distinction. One Merriam-Webster's Dictionary defintion is as follows:

relationship: "*...the way in which two or more people, groups, countries, etc., talk to, behave toward, and deal with each other...*" [4]

There is also a definition that is more about a connection:

relationship: '*...the way in which two or more people or things are connected...*" [5]

The reason for calling this out is not to state that there is no connection between love and relationships but rather, one does not require the other. The first definition of relationship states that the entities talk to, behave toward, and deal with "each other". This at least implies a two-way relationship. Love does not require a two-way relationship. Love does not depend on or even look for anything in return, including love. Love is one way. It creates a different type of relationship when it is two-way but the existence of two-way does not define love, it defines a relationship.

People and Things You Love

Subjects of love can include:
- Loving a special person (in love)
- Loving a close relative
- Loving friends
- Loving people/humanity
- Loving yourself
- Loving animals
- Loving food
- Loving activities
- Loving life

Part 1: The Fundamentals

Let's take a little time to explore some of these subjects of love.

Loving a special person – This is probably the most obvious, frequent usage and meaning of the word. There are of course various types of people and relationships between people; all can include love. This usage of love in regard to love for a special person is often referred to as being *in love*. This is the person that you are more likely to tell that you love them. You are also more likely to realize that you would do anything for them and choose their wellbeing over yours. While this type of relationship can be very complex, in its healthy state, this is the most straightforward concept of love. Having that person that you cherish, that you want to be with, that you are not sure what you would do without, is clear dedication. It is not about the potential dependency, that some may fear; rather, it is about the engulfed heartfelt dedication, happiness, and comfort that this type of love brings. There are times that this is the only thing that matters.

The phrase "in its healthy state" is specifically called out because there are relationships, or times within a relationship, that are not healthy or are not what they were thought to be and when that happens, these characteristics are probably not there. In the healthy state of this type of relationship there would be a two-way feeling of love. I don't want to come across as negative but this is a prime example to emphasize; this statement about two-way love is about the relationship. Love and relationship is not synonymous. Love can still exist with a one-way direction. Think about early on in a relationship; did one person love the other before it was mutual? It is very possible. There may be relationships where one person does not even know about the other's love for them. It does not diminish the reality of the love one bit; in fact, it provides for a very clean definition. Again, this is not referring to the relationship.

In a case where there is mutual love between two people, It might be more precise to talk about two individual loves rather than shared love or mutual love because there can be a tendency to start putting expectations on one or the other and the love that puts another first has no expectations or prerequisites. In this sense, love can only be defined as "one-way".

Loving a relative – This does not have to be exclusive to blood relatives but applies to anyone in the category of *family*, however they became family. There is a bond and a commitment to one another. This is certainly far different than the *in love* aspect of love. In this subject of love, there is love for your mother and father, your sister or brother, your daughter or son, and grandparents and cousins. You may see that the sense of family gets thinner the further you move from center in most cases, but there are exceptions to everything; parents and children that do not get along, siblings that fight and third cousins that are very close. Regardless, they are family and there is consideration given to them because of that fact. There is a sense of belonging that feels like nothing else. This sense of belonging not only brings warmth and comfort, but also a commitment to defend. You may have that feeling because of a common bond that emerges in a situation where you are defending them; you are also defending yourself, because you are defending the family.

Loving friends – There are special relationships that can form between friends. Some friends may feel closer than family but the feeling and connection is different. It is *entirely* based on choice, commonality, trust, adventure, or whatever else brought you together. Even though, in some cases, friends may feel closer than some family members, it is different. You may go to a friend to vent about the family that you love, but you may be less likely to go to family to vent about a friend.

Friends are also more likely to change than family. Of course, as with everything else, there are exceptions. Think of the friends that you have had in your life and how many are still friends; why do you think some may no longer be considered friends? It is most likely not because you decided they were not your friends anymore, but rather because life happened and people moved and changed the circles in which they live. Friends don't have family reunions and aunt Mary to hold the connections together. Of those true friends of the past, wouldn't it be great to be in touch? Social media has certainly had an impact on that to make it easier, but social media has its pros and cons.

At this point you might wonder why we would separate the special person, the relatives, friends, and even God, which we have not talked about yet. One reason is that most people think about them differently and they are called out as separate subjects of love or even different types of love. In the definition of love that we are working with, there is no difference called out based on the subjects of love. Before you disagree or are even offended by that, let me again remind that you that love is not a relationship. Your relationship is different with your kids, or sister, or spouse, or God but when you take the relationship out and just talk about love in the sense of a commitment and willingness to put the other above yourself, how can you distinguish the difference? In trying to do so, you may find yourself defining priorities rather than differences, as difficult as that may seem.

Even though love as a fundamental will have very broad impact on your life, it will likely be a rare occasion that a forced prioritization situation will arise, but at some point it will. This does not change the definition of love as a foundational component and it does not mean that you need to sit and prioritize all of the loves in your life. Since love-based decisions will likely utilize other fundamentals and the context of the situation, forcing prioritization of all the loves in your life prior to the situation would be counterproductive. If prioritization is needed, the priorities will very likely change based on the situation. We will talk more about prioritization in the Life's Realities section.

Loving people/humanity – This might look like the catchall; it is not. It may be a different category of love. You may have heard people say "I just love people", or "I care about everyone", or "I'm a *people person*". It is not the words, but the actions as with all love. When you think of an action that you might take, is there consideration for the impact to the people that you don't know?

If loving humanity is a different category of love, how is it distinguished from the other subjects of love already presented? One way might be that there is no possibility of it being two-way, but we have already eliminated that as being a relationship concept, not love. It could be that there is not a specific face to the object of the love but I recall nothing from the definitions about love needing a face as a target. It is a target that you can put before yourself for the benefit of that target. At the core definition, there is no visible difference.

So far, all of these targets of love do not change the meaning or execution of love. We have discovered that a relationship is not the same as love, which is contrary to the common assumption. Before moving on to the rest of the list, I want to call out one aspect that was mentioned earlier in the definitions of love having something to do with sex. It is certainly great when the two are related but lust is not love. That does not mean that I think that all sex is lust but sex and love can exist independent of each other just as love and relationships can.

You probably have noticed that hard lines have been drawn between words and their definitions. This is essential to communication, understanding, consistency and being able to identify and live a core set of fundamentals. Simplification of fundamentals and principles is an important part of consistency. Of course, love is complex and recognizing the complexity while embracing the simplicity allows for a healthy observation of not just love, but every aspect and event in life.

Part 1: The Fundamentals

All of the subjects of love that we have covered thus far fall into one category of love; the love of people and God across various types of relationships. I want to reiterate that *love is not defined by a relationship* or the by type of a relationship. This category may start to bring in to question the use of the word love and that is okay. The term *love* would be considered overused based on this definition. It also is important to understand the realities of the use of the word, address them and put them in perspective. Since I mentioned God again, there is probably a need to say a little more. Some may react to the comments about love being the same (in this definition) with our spouse, parents, and friends. It is even more likely that some may be offended by the statement that it also includes God. Love is a reason for decisions and that love, regardless of target, is still a reason for action. Of course, your relationship is unique with different people and with God. The expectation of getting nothing in return might be even more difficult for some with God because people turn to God *for* something. People pray for *something*. That, in no way, means that praying for something is inherently bad or selfish. Before someone gets defensive about this topic, please understand that love is only one of four of the fundamentals. Some subjects may lean more toward another fundamental and this topic, as with others, will require a combination of the fundamentals. Please stick with me. On we go to another category of love.

Loving yourself – Some will say that you have to love yourself before you can love others. While that is a good wellness statement, it may not be true in this regard. A major part of the definition of love is to put others before you. It is certainly not healthy to lack love and respect for yourself, but there are a fair amount of people that have very low self-esteem that regularly do very selfless things. I want to interject a brief implementation concept of balance. It has been inferred, but explore the concept of love as it relates to the willingness to put another before yourself and the love for self, which comes first? Great question but also somewhat of a trick question. The two are inherently contradictory; putting others before yourself and putting you first. This is where other fundamentals and operational principles influence the outcome. It is also why loving yourself is the result of all fundamentals rather than a fundamental itself. In the opening, one of the potential impacts and results of using the fundamentals was self-esteem. This takes on the pattern of an endless cyclical loop of improving life for you and those impacted by you.

Therefore, loving yourself is a category unto itself as it describes a result of all fundamentals rather than a fundamental used to make decisions. Both your self-esteem and self-respect enable more confidence and ease of using the fundamentals. When you better understand who you are, how you make decisions, and how you live your life, you are better able to appreciate and respect who you are and be comfortable with your decisions, and on the circle goes.

Loving animals – Now we have moved away from people relationships and people in general to other objects. Granted, these are still subjects of love with which you have a relationship and it may include a form of passion. There are many people that are more emotional about animals than they are about people. I am not going to try to explain that but it is certainly a fact; they treat their pet as a child; they cry over mistreatment and they would adopt a houseful of animals if they could. The same people may not cry over the bad things happening to people on the news or give any consideration of adopting kids. These are not judgment statements. It is a realization of a type of love that is real.

Loving food, activities and other objects – These are all different but they have something in common. Love of objects and activities is more a method of communicating your desire for and appreciation of *things*. Can you love food or music? Much of the time it is for your pleasure and when you turn that love of an object into giving to others, it falls into the other *person* categories such as doing it for a friend or for humanity. A good test in this case is whether the target of the love can receive the love. Love, for the purpose of a fundamental, must be *able* to be received even if it is not acknowledged or recognized.

Loving life – If there were to be a category of love that is a summary or culmination of all of the loves, this would be it. Making the most of every day. Having the appreciation for the wonder of life. Contributing what you can to the benefit of others. Living *right*. Living right implies that there is a right and wrong way to live and I believe that there is. That does not mean that there is only one *right* way and one *wrong* way. Since this topic is about love, if you live with love in your heart, you will likely be living right. You may make mistakes, but everybody makes mistakes. That is far different than living with a purpose that has another intent.

In applying the concept that love is action rather than emotion, it is important to note that actions have consequences and that lack of action is an action. Actions cannot be avoided. This does not mean that you control all of the impacts and consequences of your actions. You will not even know many of the consequences of those actions. The smallest action can have the biggest impacts that are never known. Very large actions may not have the desired specific impact, but the residual and related impacts that roll through the world because of your actions can be profound. I have so many personal examples that have come my way, but most of the cause and effects will forever remain unknown. Having love in your heart and soul along with the other fundamentals that provide guidance to your decisions is all that you can do. If you take an action out of love with expectations of what you will receive in return, you are probably looking in the wrong place or in the wrong way.

Giving love has no expectations of return or control of the outcome. Your intent is all that you own.

Since we have focused so much on actions, I want to point out some more specifics. Some that know me a *little* might consider me to be somewhat of a curmudgeon that questions most everything and everyone and therefore not much of a loving person. Love does not equate to trust or intelligence, it does not remove the ability to use other inputs in your assessments, nor does it force you to be stupid. There is information that lies before us and it is in our, and everyone's, best interest not to ignore it. Asking questions of people or challenging people does not mean that you do not have love in your heart. Likewise, the fundamental of love does not equate to blind trust. Everyone has at least heard, if not experienced, the term of tough love. In other words, doing what you believe is the best for the one that you love in spite of how difficult it may be for you and the one you love. You should gather the facts, be observant and execute in the best interest of your loved ones. This execution does not equate to control, which we will cover later.

The concept of tough love or finding the "best interest" will intersect with other fundamentals. There will be times where the line between the fundamentals of love, believing, having hope, and honor will meet, and there is not always an obvious synergy or a distinct separation of them. Life is complex and these are fundamentals rather than a science or an explicit roadmap to all of life's events. We can, however, be armed with some basics in which to ground ourselves. Reducing very complex emotions and inputs into buckets of fundamentals can aid in the ability to comprehend and address some of the complexities of life.

Part 1: The Fundamentals

Conclusions of Love

It is clear that people use the word *love* to mean many different things and for many different reasons. We started with definitions and then explored the people and things that you can love. The conclusion from this exercise of examining the very broad use of the term love is that there is limited use within the definition of fundamentals. There is, in fact, one single category derived from all of the subjects of love that is relevant to the concept of fundamentals. Some may say this is "cheating" by eliminating lots of things from scope. That is exactly the point, the purpose of simplification, and the use of fundamentals. Summarizing the subjects of love into categories is important to the simplification of the very complex and powerful subject of love.

The summaries are listed below:
1. **There are subjects that are able to receive:** this is the most important and relevant category to the fundamentals of life. The sub-categories within this category include all of the various people in all of the various relationships, humanity as a whole, God, and animals. Animals may be a bit of a gray area as being able to receive love but there are two primary reasons that I will include animals. Whether they are in or out, they will prioritize during implementation and, most importantly, these are my fundamentals so I get to define them. The return of love is not a requirement as we have discussed; it is just an observation of the commonality of the targets in this category. Identifying traits of a summary category is an important factor in simplifying the fundamentals and making them relevant to our life.
2. **Loving yourself:** This category stands on its own because it is an internal feeling of self-respect that is extremely important

to your wellbeing and your life. It can have an impact on how much you are willing and able to execute any of the categories of love and any of the fundamentals. It is not, however, the action of prioritizing the target before yourself. Yes, you could argue that you can receive the love or gift and therefore should be in the first category. In a practical and superficial example; say you gave yourself 10 dollars, what did you accomplish and can you receive something that you already had? Loving yourself is truly an internal process and recognition of yourself. As stated earlier, loving yourself is a result of using fundamentals and is an enabler to making fundamentals more effective. This category is therefore not included in the love fundamental.

3. **The objects that are loved:** This is a very broad category. Loving objects (such as food) is fine to communicate your appreciation and desire for an object but it is really irrelevant to love in the context of the fundamentals of life. Certainly, objects that you love bring you pleasure and pleasure is a meaningful aspect of life but not a fundamental for making the *important* decisions. For example, your love of cheesecake may be the reason that you decide on cheesecake over chocolate cake but these are not likely the types of decisions that define who you are. In addition, if your own pleasure was to be one of the categories of the love fundamental, it would be in direct conflict with the current definition of love. Therefore, this category is eliminated from scope.

We spent a fair amount of time examining the various subjects of love, and clarifying *important* decisions, in order to find the appropriate simplified scope of love as a fundamental. As a result, we have a further verified definition of love and a significantly reduced scope.

Part 1: The Fundamentals

Why not just say that love is giving? It is giving in the context of the willingness to prioritize others over you; giving of yourself. The gifts can be anything including something as small as a phone call or a smile, to more dramatic gifts such as money or even donating organs. The importance of the gift is not measured by the size of the gift. There is something more about the giving that makes it love. The giving has an impact on *you*; it was a choice of prioritization. Is the gift of one hundred dollars to a charity from a billionaire so they can get a tax deduction a gift of love?

Effort has been made to find simplification and clarity in the tuning of the definition of love for the purpose of understanding a personal foundation, yet there will still be complexity. You will find with all of the love that you have to share and all of the people that you love, that there will be situations where prioritization is inevitable. As we are wrapping up this chapter on love, I want to introduce two concepts in this context that are pervasive throughout the book.

The first concept; prioritization: The requirement for prioritization is not a circumstance that we can fully control or avoid and it is not something to run from, but rather an event to use *all* of your fundamentals to help you through your own personal prioritization. Prioritization is not something that has a rigid hierarchy that is the same through all circumstances. Fundamentals can provide a basis for decisions and prioritization, but each circumstance can be unique. We will discuss in later chapters that despite circumstances being unique for decisions and prioritizations, you can find patterns that will be helpful in the future.

Prioritizing love may seem crass or even impossible to think about. As stated previously, most of the implementations of love as a fundamental will not require it but if you are forced, how can you possibly choose, for example, one child over another?

Let me use a very simple example. One child is asking for $5 for candy and the other needs a school textbook that costs $20 (I know, cheap book). You only have $20. This giving choice falls within the fundamental of love. The point of this example is that you are not prioritizing your love of one child over another; you are prioritizing one need over another. You love both children, however, one child might not view it that way. Both children are loved and there is no picking one over the other, you are choosing what you believe to be the most beneficial giving within the context of the circumstances. This example is obviously over-simplified and most prioritizations involving love are not about money.

You might say that love alone didn't solve this example but consider the intent and purpose of the love. The intent of your gift is to have a positive impact on them vs. providing a moment of pleasure (candy). The decision is still based on love and the intended purpose.

Love was a driving factor in the decision and the context of the situation will always matter. Most situations of prioritization will require additional input (context and information), as well as the entire fabric of all of your fundamentals.

The second concept; accept your decisions: This is a concept about you. Does that seem ironic when this fundamental of love is about putting others before you? We are talking about loving others and putting them before you while using yourself as a *reason* for making a decision about love. The explanation for this is that it does not actually make the decision; it addresses a way to resolve to yourself that you had to make a decision and you made one. You can only make the best decision that you can at the time by using your fundamentals and all of the other information available to you. Other information may come forward later but it is important to *accept and believe* that you did the best at the time with the information available and your fundamentals standing by your side. This is where the cascading impact of using fundamentals comes into play and grows in its strength.

Part 1: The Fundamentals

Your ability to find inner peace is dependent upon your confidence in understanding who you are (your fundamental fabric) and that the fabric of who you are is represented by the decisions that you make. Since decisions are also dependent upon the context of the situation, the decision is only valid in that moment.

We will now continue through the rest of the fundamentals to build the fabric. As we explore the next fundamentals, we will see the relationship between fundamentals, cross-checking, and validation come into play.

Part 1: The Fundamentals

Chapter 1-3
HONOR

As with the fundamental of Love, let's start with some of the underlying ideas that spawned the conclusion of Honor as a fundamental. The ideas included integrity, honesty, consistency, respect, trust and that general concept of doing the "right thing". Some of these ideas may not be fully engulfed in Honor but determining that is part of the process. The ideas are part of who I am, so they need to find a grounding home somewhere in one or more fundamentals. Honor, by itself, may not tell you what the right thing is, your fabric will. Once you have identified the right thing, honor will hold you to it.

Starting with Merriam-Webster's definitions of honor confirmed the breadth of the word. I thought that love was a word with a lot of meanings but honor has thirteen major definitions and when you apply the distinct variations of definitions from the dictionary, there are twenty-five. Twenty-five definitions of a single word! No wonder we have a hard time communicating. Regardless, it provides a place from which to start honing the definition to our purpose of a fundamental that is manageable. Unlike other terms that have 2-4 variations of defintions, Merriam-Webster's Dictionary has almost 30 variations of the defintion of honor. I went through more of a documentation process with this term and put all of the variations into one of three categories for relativity to this book. The categories were simple; yes, no, and maybe. The following samples are the variations that fell into the yes category:

honor: *"...1b: a showing of usually merited respect ... 8a: a keen sense of ethical conduct: INTEGRITY // a man of honor ... 2a: to live up to the terms of // honor a commitment..."* [6]

Examples of other uses of honor that do not apply include:
1. "I am defending my *honor*."
2. "I had the *honor* of being selected."
3. "I was an *honor* student."
4. "I am innocent Your *Honor*."

Without going through the detail of each elimination, the general reason for elimination is that they did not fit the original ideas that brought me to *Honor* as a fundamental in the first place. I certainly did not have playing cards, golf, square dancing, awards, or titles in mind. The important part of this effort is the remaining definitions and eventually coming to a single working definition that encompasses those aspects of honor. The remaining definitions include the concepts of showing respect, ethical conduct/integrity, and living up to the terms of an agreement. There were also two maybes that were adequately covered in concept by the three variations that were selected.

The resulting definitions generally have two types, as I would expect, based on the original ideas. There is honor that is focused on you and honor that is focused on others. We will explore these types of honor in more detail, but first let's see if we can find a single working definition. We will validate that definition after we complete the details of the two types of honor. Notice we are now talking about two types rather than twenty-five and the goal is one.

Working definition:

honor: *The actions taken in a consistent and respectful way based on a set of values.*

I know that I used consistent and respect in this definition, which do not have full definitions themselves, but I believe that they are understood enough for now. The more important aspect of this definition is that it introduces the concept of a set of values. This is critical to the meaning of honor. You might ask why the values are not a fundamental if honor is dependent on them. The reason is that while you could argue that values is a *why*, the list of values can be numerous and they need a bucket to hold them. It is also true that the other fundamentals are part of values. Honor is the method by which you make the values and components of who you are actionable in a consistent and measurable way. Keep in mind that this is the initial working definition. Let's continue through the honing process and look at more detail of the two types of honor to see if we can resolve the questions and confusion around *values*.

Values, Principles, and the Concept of Right and Wrong

In doing my research for related terms, I determined that it would be easy to get wrapped up in the differences and dependencies between terms. So many definitions reference each other and use terms like ethical and moral in their definition. I tried to leave *moral* and *ethical* terms out of the working definition because it is arguably subjective and prescribes nothing. One exception where ethical may be prescriptive is ethical conduct prescribed by law but that is not the place I wanted to go. I decided that I need to go another direction after digging deep and looking at not only the circular reference across these terms, but the evolution of the meanings and philosophical debates over the terms and their relationships. I even found newspaper and magazine articles and books addressing that debate. It is not the purpose of this book to take on that debate; however, we do need to verify the working definition of honor. After sorting through the intertwined and confusing definitions of all of the terms, I finally found two of the definitions of principle in Merriam-Webster's Dictionary that get pretty close to what I was looking for in *values*; they are:

principle: *"... (1): a rule or code of conduct   (2): habitual devotion to right principles..."* [7]

From this, I know that I need to tune this definition of principle a little in order to fit into my working definition of Honor that uses values. It makes it more challenging when definitions use the word in the definition; in fact, that might break one of *my* principles.

I believe that I can leave out the second part of the definition, not only because it uses principles in the definition but because that portion is covered by Honor. The first part needs a clarification that the rules or code of conduct are yours and not those defined by someone else.

Values are not quite resolved yet because there is *Believing*, which is a fundamental yet to be discussed; it has a potential significant overlap with the concept of values.

I cannot avoid addressing the fact that I am touching on the fundamental of believing as it relates to principles. They will both be discussed in more detail in later chapters. There is a clear relationship between believing and principles but I need to make the distinction between them, even though they don't conflict. The use of the fundamentals will be intertwined; it is required to form the fabric and will become more obvious as we move along. The fundamentals also need to have purpose and definition of their own, otherwise they would be redundant.

Principles are the rules or code of conduct that define "right" for you. Let's resolve to a definition of principles that is a rule or code of conduct prescribed for oneself. You can certainly believe in those things, but you can believe in anything including love and fundamentals. Believing in things that are not focused on the process or rules covered by principles is real, and the consistency of implementation provided by honor needs to apply to those as well.

The next chapter is Believing and there is a chapter later about principles so we will see more details coming up. That will also be yet another opportunity for cross-checking and validation. As you can probably see, we need to update the working definition to the following:

honor: *The consistent actions and commitment to your principles and beliefs.*

Honor would imply that you would not lie, that you would mean what you say and uphold promises made and that all of these things are consistently executed. After all, *honor cannot be intermittent*. A leader in a corporate setting once told me that I was too *principled* to make it there. Based on the circumstances, that meant that I would say what I believed, I would not say things that I believed to be "wrong", and that I would not misrepresent the facts or myself. It was a very sad statement but an honest one and I took it as a compliment, but it was also an insight into the reality of dishonesty and deception in the world. It also is a good example that your actions have consequences, even the honorable actions. In this case, I was perfectly willing to accept the consequences, in order to be true to myself. That does not mean that I thought they were justified, or that I submitted and lost all hope.

Honor is the fundamental that can mitigate or prevent regrets. It is a major factor in achieving the most positive results from the fabric of your fundamentals, for yourself and others.

The Impact of Honor on Yourself

Honor can result in trust in yourself, but even more than that, it is how you live with yourself. It is the agreement that you have with yourself to be who you are. Those without honor will find their way around life in some form. They may have both positive and negative impacts on others' lives just like those with honor, however; there is little on which to base expectations, trust and reliability in themselves.

The cascading impacts include:
- Consistency leads to a higher level of impact on others
- Being true to you leads to a higher level of self-esteem and self-respect
- Consistency and self-respect lead to inner peace

As you can see, the description of this portion of the cascading impacts is rooted in *Honor*.

These points are focused on better results from your fundamentals but how does this type of honor help you make decisions? Getting engrained in this honorable mode is one of the most straight-forward means of impacting decisions. Straight-forward does not mean easy until it becomes engrained (a behavior rather than a thought). Consistency is not a hard concept to understand and using previous statements helps to create those patterns of reusability that we discussed earlier.

With honor, you have your basis that is your personal "moral" compass. This is not the morals imposed or judged by others; they are owned and executed by you. The more you are able to execute with honor, the more confidence you will have in yourself. You will also have a growing trust in your judgment and commitment to other aspects of decisions and your life. The difference between knowing that you are acting in a measured and consistent manner, rather than random acts and decisions, is at the core of the purpose and benefits of fundamentals.

As I have stated previously, nobody will be perfect in his or her execution. That is not a reason for despair. Having your fabric in place to provide the method and guiderails by which to measure and improve will prove well worth the effort. Over time, decisions will become easier and, in some cases, even automated (subconscious).

The Impact of Honor on Others

Honor has externalized impact on others that is undeniable unlike the internal impacts that may not be quite as evident until you experience it for yourself. This is not a self-righteous statement but rather a self-aware statement.

The two most obvious impacts on others are the respect and trust they have in you. People will understand that you are consistent, mean what you say, and are a person whose word means something. People trusting you provides feedback to you that supports your own self-respect, especially for those that may be a bit insecure and reliant on feedback from others. Your self-respect and trust in yourself, in turn, becomes evident in your actions to others. It is a wonderful loop. Respect and trust are also covered in more detail in later chapters.

An external impact that goes even further is one that creates your presence and impact when you are not there. When someone says, "I know what he or she would say", that presence is there. Even when they don't say those words, there can be a transfer of information, knowledge, and perspective that can in turn assist others with forming their principles that they will then apply, and so on, and so on… Sharing your true self is a wonderful thing.

Conclusion

We spent a *lot* of time dissecting terms in this chapter. Why all of the work and details in this chapter regarding which word to use? How important is that to life? The reason is not for the purpose of meticulous wordsmithing or just getting hung up on the details of the word. The purpose, especially true within honor, is for you to understand. If you make a statement such as the definition of honor and intend to be consistent in its execution, you better be able to explain and defend what it means. Without that you will not succeed.

It started with honor which led to values, principles, and believing, amongst others. After all of the work of honing the definitions, discussing the overlaps, and discarding the irrelevant or confusing terms, I know that I have a better understanding of the fundamental of Honor. We landed on a definition that is broad enough to include all fundamentals, principles, and beliefs and yet focused enough to understand the intent of commitment and consistency. Talking about the breadth of the definition, it brings to mind the question of whether or not we have undermined one of the major purposes of fundamentals, which is to simplify. Note, the definition allows for breadth but does not require it since the function of honor is consistency in execution. Whether you have two principles or two hundred, the purpose is the same. I did not provide guidance on the recommended number of principles or beliefs because they can grow as you are comfortable with them and as they become subconscious actions.

Nobody is perfect and judgmental scrutiny applied with force to anyone may result in someone being able to say "Ah-ha, we found you out". The exceptions are not the point; exceptions will pass. The patterns that you live will stand above the anomalies. The recognition of your beliefs and your principles that characterize your distinction between right and wrong is an essential step. Your willingness to live your life according to those convictions and defend them, even when there may be short-term personal negative impacts, is *Honor*. I know that is a mouthful but it is the essence of honor.

Honor will occasionally take courage; "courage of your convictions" as the saying goes. You may know that some may not like what you say, some may feel that you should always agree with them, and some may be in a position to take action against you. You may not get that promotion. You may not get that job. You may not win the award. You may not be the favorite parent (for a while). When you consider the fabric of your life, these likely do not fall in the category that we discussed regarding the important things and the important decisions.

Implementing your fundamentals with honor is the *long game*.

Honor brings respect to the other fundamentals and is a key supporting factor of your self-respect, which leads to inner peace.

Chapter 1-4
BELIEVING

Believing was mentioned a lot in the Honor fundamental chapter. As with other fundamentals, evidence is in the actions, but *believing* is more of a soulful state of mind in its origin than all others. In some cases, believing may have no proof or scientific conclusions and absolutely requires faith. Faith in *knowing* something that may not be able to be "proven".

Since believe(believing) is the verb, I want to also look at the noun that is belief in Merriam-Webster's Dictionary:

believe: *"...1a : to accept something as true, genuine, or real //ideals we believe in //believes in ghosts   b: to have a firm or wholehearted religious conviction or persuasion : to regard the existence of God as a fact..."* [8]

belief: *" ...a state or habit of mind in which trust or confidence is placed in some person or thing..."* [9]

The definition for both forms of the word is appropriate. The wording used between them is slightly different and they are important distinctions. One refers to true and genuine and the other refers to trust and confidence. I consider them different and both are acceptable. So far, this seems way too simple; definitions that actually work. We're not quite done yet. First, we have a lingering lack of differentiation between principles and believing, so let's attempt to resolve that.

A person can believe in many things, and for many reasons, including believing in their principles. Believing in your principles is implied by the fact they are your principles. Your principles would not exist if you did not believe them. Remember, each person can have a process and rules that are "right" to them. If you did not believe them, you would not create them. The conclusion would be different if the principles were externally imposed ethics or morals.

Why does the definition of honor call out both principles and beliefs? Why do we need to draw a distinction between principles and beliefs for use in the fundamentals? Why are principles not just part of beliefs? If the definition of belief was allowed to be so big that it would encompass everything, then we would have one fundamental and we would just state that we are what we believe. While this may be true, it is not helpful for simplification and does not provide the cross-checking and validation discussed in earlier chapters. For the purpose of fundamentals, we will recognize that the act of believing can apply to principles, but principles are distinctly specific to the rules and processes that define *right*. All of the other categories of believing will be based on something other than principles. It is time to create and look at the other categories of believing in order to be more specific than "everything other than principles". We need to do that for simplification and focus. In this case we are not so much honing the definition, but rather what the definition applies to.

Believing can tend to take on a religious tone or implication. It is a common and good example of believing but believing, in itself, is not restricted to religion or God. People can believe in a variety of things. Merriam-Webster's definition refers to ghosts, while some believe that everybody is good at heart, or that if you touch a toad you will get warts. Beliefs come from many sources and occur for various reasons. Understanding the sources is important to understanding the perspective and intensity of the belief. This discussion of these sources will further differentiate beliefs from principles.

It is also going to be important to understand the concepts of proof, evidence, facts, truth, perception and belief. I am going to go with the premise that there are three categories of beliefs other than principles. They include beliefs that are based on facts, those that are based on perceptions, and those that are based on faith. We will look at each one of them in detail to see if any can help narrow the scope. The terms related to facts, truth, and perception are discussed in much more detail in later chapters. For now, I will offer these high-level concepts for the three categories:

- Beliefs based on facts that are proven by existence and not by a statement
- Beliefs based on perceptions, which are opinions
- Beliefs are what come from within and cannot be proven or disproven

Beliefs Based on Facts

There are beliefs that that are based on facts. You believe something because the information that you have that is irrefutable. Facts should not change, other than the facts that are represented by a time factor such as, it is 3:00. The fact would have to change to it was 3:00 one minute ago. Facts are not projections or conclusions except where conclusions are proven by mathematical formulas. An example would be, if it were a fact that you have one apple and a fact that I have two apples, it is also a concluded fact that *we* have three apples. From this, an important observation, or perception, would be that there are relatively few actual facts compared to the other types of beliefs.

Beliefs Based on Perceptions

This category of beliefs touches on terms such as observation, opinion, trust, rumor, and even stupidity. This is the most dangerous category of beliefs and has the risk of overshadowing the other categories and even all fundamentals. This category includes the things that people have given little or no thought, yet still believe. This category is prevalent in social media and is a key factor in "mob" mentality. Perceptions that are believed without vetting are opinions that can take on a groundswell of emotion that has little to do with beliefs. From this type of belief come things like prejudice. They are things that are heard in passing, or from a friend of a friend, or "they just believe that". This category, for the most part, contains beliefs that could be proven or disproven if the time was taken to look at them, but that has not been done.

The use of the word *belief* as representing an opinion is technically correct, but it leaves that belief open to discussion. New evidence may surface that may cause the conclusion that formed the opinion to change. Change works well for an *opinion*. Sometimes people will take statements beyond the recognition that they are opinions and turn them into their personal facts, even when there is irrefutable evidence to the contrary; even when that evidence is *fact*. Giving no thought to the belief or turning opinion into fact is where the danger lies. This is now the transition to the third and most relevant category.

Part 1: The Fundamentals

Beliefs Based on Faith

Based on the discussion of perception, this does not mean that things that cannot be proven or become *fact*, should not be believed. Of course, people will believe in things that cannot be *proven* and they should not have to prove everything. When someone talks about believing, and especially when they talk about *faith*, the first thing to come to mind for most is religion, God or anything spiritual. It is an extremely good example of those things that fall into this category of faith-based beliefs, but it is not the only one.

So, what type of things do people try to prove that cannot truly be proven and will ultimately fall to *believing*? Religion is one and I am certain that some will take the position that it can be proven. I would be glad to have that conversation but it is called faith for a reason. I want to remind you that it also means that it cannot be disproven. The other major type of faith-based beliefs consists of things in the future. These are things that may or may not happen, things that may or may not be created or discovered. Some may believe that there is life on other planets, or that the world will be flooded by water, etc. At some point, people believed that the world was flat. There was no proof of that unless you had been to the edge and obviously nobody had done that; yet, it was a widely accepted "fact". I do not want this to sound like I am saying that you should only believe in things that can be proven; far from it. I am trying to set the parameters that constitute a belief of faith that cannot be proven or disproven with everything that exists today. Understand that all beliefs have the strength of conviction and have the possibility of being proven right or wrong in the future. The possibility of being proven wrong should not be a deterrent of believing. Without beliefs and convictions, many things in life would never happen.

Believing Intensity

A belief does align with one's own perception of reality and as such *implies* an expectation of reality or truth. Since slightly real might be considered analogous to slightly pregnant, we could conclude that there is also not a concept of a slight belief. If there is not a slight belief, then levels of belief do not make sense either. Either you believe or you don't. "I kind of believe" or "I believe a little" are slightly odd statements. If there are degrees of belief, how does that align with the intensity of a belief?

For many beliefs, there is an associated level of intensity or passion. Passion, in this regard, is both admirable and dangerous. Intensity and passion are not part of the belief or a grading of the belief; they are emotions that surround the belief. We have discussed the danger of the perception category but passion adds even more risk. Passion, or intensity of the commitment to a perception, not only make it less likely to be able to hear truth if it comes along, it creates a vulnerability. People will use it against you as a method of manipulation. They will either use the passion that exists to manipulate other actions or find other passions in your life to associate to an opinion. Simple examples: "That person is a cheater", "That person is a liar", or "That person can't be trusted". They would all be said with a great deal of emotion of course and the more you can relate to having been negatively impacted by cheaters, liars, or untrustworthy people, the more likely you are to *believe*. You might also be influenced by who told you this, as well as the number of people that told you or who also believes. Social media is prime for this behavior.

Because of manipulation or just social pressure it is important that you look for verification, validation, or anything that gives you something to stand on prior to adopting and promoting someone else's opinion as your own belief. Not doing so, puts you in a position where you are dramatically wandering from your fundamentals and starting to make decisions based on very little, and that is putting it very mildly.

It is not only perceptions that are impacted by passion. Faith-based passion is also susceptible to the passion impact but in a much different way. Faith, as we have discussed, cannot be proven or disproven but the believer takes it as fact due to faith, which is just fine. That is the nature of faith. The reason that I even mention it in the context of faith is that some people attempt to use it as an argument against faith. Being aware of that position is just one of those realities of life to be aware of. The position is that passionate faith results in hatred, war, and killing. The holy wars! It is a fact that many major wars were created or enhanced based on religious "passion". The more appropriate word might be zealot, but in this case it's in the same category. They must not have had their fundamentals in place. That was supposed to be funny and also true.

Once again, it is really not the faith or belief that has degrees of intensity but the emotion and commitment that gets attached. Two tests of this behavior are worth looking at:

1. Can you still listen to someone else with a different opinion or even facts that might challenge your opinion?
2. Have you entered a place where others must believe what you believe or they are wrong?

There is a reason that *right and wrong* are separated out into *principles*. Imposing your right and wrong on others steps into *control* which is one of those life realities in Part 2 of this book.

Believing Summary

Can people change what they believe in? Of course they can, but the type of belief that is rooted in facts is far different in its character than the belief that cannot be proven or disproven. What is in and what is out and what is something else?

Principles: You can, and in fact must, believe in your personal principles by definition. They have a home with the Honor fundamental so they will not be duplicated with Believing.

Facts: As some might say, "Facts is facts". You can and should question facts and verify them for yourself but once they are established as fact, which does not come easy, they are facts. You can believe in facts but they already have a name so they will remain facts. Facts are also not called out as a fundamental. They absolutely can contribute to decisions but they are not your fabric. They are part of the context of a situation to which you apply the fundamentals.

Perception: The most volatile of all categories. These opinions can change, and likely should change, based on ever-changing circumstances. We also discussed the various risks associated with this category. Calling them and treating them as perceptions or opinions rather than beliefs would certainly be a more accurate and probably safer statement. This is not a category to be a grounding point for the important decisions in your life. Perception is therefore not part of the scope of Believing for our purpose.

Faith: As it turns out, all categories of believing have been eliminated from scope except faith. Faith is an easy one to get confused with perception because some would argue that it is an opinion. The key difference is that items of faith cannot be proven or disproven. They are far less likely to be disrupted by information or facts because, by definition, they cannot be proven or disproven.

Part 1: The Fundamentals

I know that I have repeated that statement multiple times but it is critical to keeping the scope in check. These are the relevant beliefs that cause believing to be fundamental. It is a special group of beliefs whose criterion does not fit in another place. For some it is a major part of who they are and for some it is minor. Regardless of where it is for you today, it likely needs a home as a piece of who you are. We now have three of four fundamentals.

Part 1: The Fundamentals

Chapter 1-5
HOPE

Since we have made it through 3 of the 4 fundamentals, you would likely expect that the last one would fill in any gaps. That should be the case. At a high level, you have *love* driving many of your actions, you have *honor* providing your integrity and consistency across all fundamentals and principles, and you have your *beliefs* acknowledging those things in your life that are not covered by love, principles, or the ever-changing external information. Many additional decisions will likely be driven by a combination of fundamentals. What is missing? What about those situations where you fall short of a belief and you don't have supporting facts but your principles tell you something is *right*?

Let's start with a cliché. "Anything is possible". That is not exactly *hope*; in fact, it might sound closer to despair for some; "Anything is possible but I'm not going to count on it or even hold out hope". Hope can certainly, as with most things, come from various motivators. Some may say that strong enough confidence in hope shifts to another

foundational component of believing. I do not see it that way. I see hope as being either *on* or *off*. There are three options for hope:
1. Your hope has been fulfilled so there is no longer a need for hope (off)
2. You persist the hope and continue action toward the hope (on)
3. You let hope go, so hope does not exist (off)

Hope is much more closely related to persistence in its implementation. One would have to wonder if hope and desire are even more closely related. I believe they are very closely related but they are not the same thing; someone can have desire but give up hope which is not a good state to be in. The starving artists are classic examples of people with hope. This is an easy example to use but understand that people that are ill, have turmoil in their life, or are watching over others, are more acute situations where hope is a key factor.

As we did with other fundamentals, let's look to the dictionary but this time Noah Webster's 1828 dictionary definition:

hope: *"A desire of some good, accompanied with at least a slight expectation of obtaining it, or a belief that it is obtainable. hope differs from wish and desire in this, that it implies some expectation of obtaining the good desired, or the possibility of possessing it..."* [10]

I like to go to the dictionary as a starting point for definitions of words, but it is not uncommon that I find some challenges or issues where my own perception or logical thinking is required to get some form of precision regarding the words. This definition points out that a hope is different than a wish, and I believe that it is, but it also uses the term of slight expectation. To me, this term is irrelevant, similar to being slightly pregnant; what the heck does that mean? If you look up expectation, it will tell you that it is a belief. Now we are entwined in the fundamental of believing which will take us in a circle of no clear distinction between hope, expectation (slight), and believing. No wonder we have a hard time communicating. Let me clarify for the purpose of this book and its foundational aspects where it is important to understand the distinction.

Expectation has nothing to do with hope. As stated previously, desire and a wish can exist but hope can be abandoned, so they are not the same. Appropriate use of believing in this case is the *belief in the possibility*. Here is where the line lies between Hope and Believing. Belief has no question of outcome and hope has belief in the possibility and worthiness of the persistence to keep trying. We drew a pretty hard line on believing for a reason. The major reason was to try to draw clean lines between fact, perception and belief. In drawing those lines, there is an important scenario where I see a gap. I know that there are things that I hope will happen and, under the definition of believing, I cannot say that I believe that they will. It is also much stronger than a wish or I would stop making decisions based on hope.

Some may challenge this perspective. Many have asked me how I can keep trying when the results are so contrary to the desire. This is *not* like the quote that is most frequently attributed to Albert Einstein, "Insanity is doing the same thing over and over again and expecting different results." [11] It is continually trying every variation and every angle that can be expressed to try to achieve a desired outcome. You may be trying to get a break as an entertainer, or to convince someone to understand your position, or to beat an illness, or anything that can be imagined with an effort put toward achieving your objective. I guess you could argue that whether or not you do anything, you can still have hope. I could "hope" that a million dollars will land in my lap just because. I would not consider that hope. Maybe it's desire or dreaming but remember the premise for these fundamentals, they are based on actions. They are actionable. What will I do to make a million dollars land in my lap? Is it *reasonably* possible?

I am going to share a personal experience where hope was with me for many years. This is similar to the starving artist but I did not have the starving part to push me in a direction. I was in a position where I was hired to do a job and the outline of the job and goals of the job were of great interest to me. They would provide me with a sense of value and accomplishment if they could be achieved. Even more than that, the goals were doing things that I saw as providing a great deal of benefit by doing the right thing. The right thing, as I saw it, was part of the description of the position. What I found was that when I attempted to achieve the goal (doing my job) my efforts were rejected. Not only were my efforts rejected, others were rewarded for blocking the efforts and even doing the opposite of the goal. Okay, this was frustrating and confusing for a while and I am not going to take you through the number of times and examples that I experienced those behaviors and results.

The important aspect is that each experience like that caused a reassessment of my personal perspective and provided context and input into future decisions regarding my job. I think that many people can relate to that type of feeling whether it be regarding a job or relationships or other aspects of life. If you are not appreciated or are even rejected, how much will you put into it and how long will you stay?

I looked at things like how I might have misunderstood the goal, queried others for their opinion, and reassessed the information to develop a *new* approach. There are so many factors to obtaining the desired outcome in most situations and those factors cannot be ignored. Understanding language and goals during communication is critical.

To cut this personal experience short, I tried for years and eventually gave up hope. My hope was lost when I realized that the people that told me they wanted something, clearly did not want it. Their motivation for saying they wanted it was driven by something other than actually wanting it. My other fundamentals prevented me from going where they truly wanted to go, so I left.

If everybody walked away from an initial rejection or disappointment, there would be no reason for hope. On the flip side, this is also not the mentality of "never give up". At some point hope may be abandoned; you can still wish but no longer consider it possible. For me, it changed my decisions so that I didn't repeat the exact same behavior and tried various approaches considering the changing environment such as changes in senior management. Finally my personal line was crossed.

Hope requires some level of personal and reasonable logic. Since reasonable is completely subjective and *personal* emphasizes that fact, the line will be different for everybody but regardless of where the line lies, there should be a line. That being said, hope is not factual or scientific but it does, and should, represent a conclusion that is feasible and for which you have taken some action to achieve. The action that you take is not defined in such a way that forces you to do particular things. If you believe that those things can have an impact, you are taking action. We have just identified another relationship between hope and believing. If you believe in prayer, you likely do not believe that all prayers have the outcome that you want. That is where you can believe in prayer and hope for the outcome.

I *believe* that this book will help someone. I have a *desire* that this book will help a lot of people and I have *hope* that it will. In order to try to make my hope feasible, I am trying to consider various aspects within the book that might ring true for more people and I am consulting with others for their feedback and perspective. I will also need a marketing strategy for more exposure. Doing those two things, and few others, gives me reason to hope.

I "published" another book nine years ago and I am still working the hope related to it. My original expectations were met in that I would give the book to some close friends and relatives and some of them would read it. Expectations were not high. My hope was that more would read it and some would benefit from it. I did not have a distribution model to go beyond friends and family and my printer went out of business. I found a new publisher and have an outline of a distribution model. My expectations are still low but I have hope for more people seeing it and benefiting from it.

There are no time constraints on action but let me add a little more guidance to *reasonableness*. There is an obligation of reasonable effort so as to not play games with the effort. I will use what may be a stupid scenario but hopefully it makes the point. Let's say you pray that you are able to get to work on time tomorrow for a big meeting. You cannot control the traffic but you can watch for it. You cannot control the weather but you can be prepared. If it snows 10" and you get stuck in your driveway because you didn't shovel your driveway, you probably can't claim that your action failed or that you even took reasonable action. This speaks to accountability. Many things cannot be controlled but remember that taking no action is a decision and is in itself an action with consequences. The point of this is not to be judgmental or to put pressure on you to think of and do everything, but rather to set the boundaries for claiming hope and making it actionable.

When talking about "believing in the possibility", the key word is *possible* when it pertains to hope. Hope as a fundamental would require the willingness to continue to take some form of action because of that possibility. Your motivation to continue can come from various places including from hope itself. Yes, hope can motivate itself. You might even say that in the context of hope being actionable, hope *is* motivation. There is a word that has been referred to a few times in this chapter but it has not been discussed. The word is goal. Goals are one of the concepts and terms like principles that could be so broad as to encompass everything. That is not the intent or purpose of using the term and I will not declare it as a fundamental because it is the result of all fundamentals; it is a decision that you make. We have just identified another example of the circular benefits of the fundamentals, the nature of your fabric, and the power that it has to be self-sustaining.

When you know something is the right thing to do and you believe in possibilities of the right thing to do, you can continue to take varied action with hope for a different result. This is not insanity. This is the power of your fabric enabling the power of you. Goals can be formed by any combination of your fundamentals, in other words by your fabric. Without hope, all of the love, honor and beliefs could rapidly fall short of the goal; this is the gap that hope fills.

Part 1: The Fundamentals

Chapter 1-6
SUMMARY OF FUNDAMENTALS

In this chapter, we will review the conclusions that we discovered while defining the fundamentals. We will also begin to explore external impacts, some implementation strategies, and look closer at the fabric and the fundamental *circle*.

General Philosophy Sidebar

The concept of using *fundamentals* is a method of simplification by using a process to understand and define yourself. Your fundamentals are then used as a foundation for making decisions. This approach has personal benefits that we have discussed including inner peace and so much more.

This approach may irritate some that follow a variety of other philosophies and/or theories. There are some philosophies that will be in conflict with the approach of fundamentals purely on the premise that we cannot make decisions and there are some philosophies that will be in conflict with the fundamentals that I have selected. A point to take from this is that there is no *fact* of the correct philosophy. There are a great deal of opinions and perceptions and for many it falls into a category of *belief*. For those that have a belief of their philosophy, there will likely be a great deal of passion, as they will see their philosophy as fact.

There are so many philosophies but I want to give a very brief overview of a few of them as examples. Before you get too concerned, this is not turning into a deep dark study of philosophies. I believe that it is helpful to understand the world around you and that many people subscribe to a wide variety of philosophies and you will encounter them in your daily life. It is real easy to close off the recognition of how diverse people's philosophies (beliefs) are. I am not going to try to convince you that any of them are bad or wrong, or right for that matter. I am also fairly sure that anyone that has strong convictions conflicting with this approach will not read this book for any reason other than to say that it is wrong.

I am not approaching the fundamentals of life as a belief. The concept of the fundamentals, by its design, is a concept whose details are intended to grow with us and continually be tuned with the knowledge and wisdom that we gain through life. The particular fundamentals selected are of the nature of a personal philosophy. Don't let that be disturbing that you are creating or subscribing to a philosophy. According to the philosophy department at the University of Florida, "In a broad sense, philosophy is an activity people undertake when they seek to understand fundamental truths about themselves..." [12] This is exactly what we have been doing so this just puts a label on it.

I do not profess to be the authority of various philosophies, so I will present the following examples as opinions that I have gained based on information that I have read. I encourage you to do your own research on these philosophies if you are interested.

Part 1: The Fundamentals

Determinism / Fatalism: These theories are similar in that they both believe that we have no choice in the outcome of our life. Fatalism's position is that, regardless of what we do, we will end up in the same place (it is our fate). Determinism's position is that we actually have no choice in any event in our life; we have no choice in anything that we do because it is the effect of something that happened previously. Everything is a chain of events and once it is started, there is no changing it. That would mean that I had no choice in writing this book or the words in it and you had no choice in deciding to read it. I clearly do not believe these philosophies, as this book is about making decisions and using the fundamentals for doing so. If these philosophies were true, this book and its concepts would be of no value.

A major newspaper reported the results of a survey saying that 52% of Americans believe in fate. It is important to note that they did not define how the question was asked or what people believe to be fate. Some practitioners of psychology may state that believing in fate removes responsibility and the pressure to make the *right* decision.

Hedonism: The purpose of life is one's own pleasure or happiness. This is likely not in conflict with the concept of fundamentals but would certainly be in conflict with the fundamentals that I have selected. In its most extreme form (libertinism), there would likely be a singular fundamental of one's own pleasure, which would break one of the guidelines for fundamentals.

Nihilism: Nihilism is described as the rejection of all religious and moral principles, in the belief that life is meaningless. In an escalated form of extreme skepticism, nihilism maintains that nothing in the world has a real existence. This philosophy would certainly be in conflict with the fundamentals that I have selected and likely would reject the concept of the fundamentals used for decisions because nothing matters.

Stoicism: Stoicism is associated with bringing mental toughness. Many seem to see this philosophy as a method to "make it" through tough times, but from a broad brush it seems to be addressing both the highs and lows in the removal of all emotion. A description of ancient Greek stoicism states that it teaches the development of self-control and fortitude as a means of overcoming destructive emotions.

Relationalism: Relationalism, in a broader sense, applies to any philosophical theory that gives importance to the relational nature of reality. In a narrower sense, relationalism refers to the theory of reality that interprets the nature, and even existence of things only in terms of their relationality to other things. In other words, there are no self-standing entities. This theory, in its broad sense, is relevant to the concept of relationships between fundamentals and the creation of a fabric.

Relativism: Relativism sounds like relationalism but its implementation of relationships is different. Relativism can be applied to many aspects and may be referred to as negative relativism, positive relativism, ethical relativism, moral relativism, and more. The general idea is that there is no *truth* or right or wrong and everything is specific to its context. This would not conflict with the framework for fundamentals because the framework allows for personalization. I have even made the statement that "everything is relative" but I would not take it to this level. In my opinion, it would be hard to have a belief that you believed could not be the *truth*. There are chapters regarding relativity, truth, good, and evil later in this book that will further define my position on these topics. This is also a good example of continuously tuning your personal philosophy. I will be changing my statement regarding everything is relative to further explain the context in which it applies for me, which is primarily for communication. Regardless of what I think, this is a real theory/philosophy.

Taoism: It is stated that can take both a religious and philosophical form. I find it personally hard to distinguish the difference. In this case Tao means a road, path, or way; the way in which one does something. It may be seen as a method, doctrine, or principle. The basic belief of Taoism is that "Tao" is the origin and law of all things in the universe. Tao is not a deity. There seems to be four basic doctrines of the Tao (Dao) but I am not going to go into that level of detail for the purpose of this overview.

I want to reiterate that the purpose for this overview is not to provide teachings in these philosophies but rather to recognize their existence.

Altruism: Altruism is described as the belief and practice of selfless concern for the well-being of others. This is one that some may say is representative of what I am proposing in the four fundamentals. That is not the way that I see it; however, it is far closer than some of the other philosophies thus far. The concepts of fundamentals can support any theory that believes in our ability to choose and make decisions. The derived definition of the love fundamental is very close to the meaning of altruism. I would therefore conclude that those that do not ever make altruist decisions do not believe in love and are likely not capable of it. Would you remove love from the list?

The aspect of the fundamental concept and my specific fundamentals that does not fit purely in altruism is the fact that love is not the only fundamental. We have talked about the creation of the fabric and we will even more. We have also talked about the impact of context, priorities and other information available at the time. One of the benefits of the fundamental concept is your own personal inner peace. I do not believe that our own inner peace would be part of a pure altruistic approach to life.

Buddhism: Buddhism can also have a form that is either religious or philosophical. There are also many variations of Buddhism. One thing that seems to be common across all variations is the concept of *Four Noble Truths*. Buddhism also has a number of precepts and rules that prescribe *morality*. Amongst its other concepts is the idea of suffering and its ultimate cessation. It is probably the most complex to summarize of the philosophies that are listed. There is nothing I can see that would prevent it from fitting into the fundamental concept; however, its prescribed process, rules, and definitions of morals and right, may have its own *path* without the fundamental concept. I use the word path because that is another concept in Buddhism called the Noble Eightfold Path, and the eight all begin with the word "right".

Philosophy summary: The examples are just a few of the philosophies that are out there. These examples were not selected to make a point. They were the result of various searches looking for prominent or top examples of philosophies. When it comes down to it, a philosophy is a belief. Philosophies, just like beliefs, can take on many forms. Some are religious, some are ethical, some are behavioral, some are positive, and some are negative. Specific religions such as Christianity and atheism were not called out. They are both beliefs but not necessarily in the mainstream of what would be considered *philosophies*. That being said, the existence of God is always a major and passionate topic in the philosophy forums. There is a very strong presence of people that do not believe that there is a God and that religions are a hoax, mostly on the basis that they cannot "prove" it. Lack of proof seems to equate to these self-proclaimed logical people as proof of the negative. Many of them will call people stupid and other names while claiming that "they know the facts" and *"they* are right". When I see people claiming to know facts that cannot possibly be known, they have lost the argument and credibility for me.

For some, a philosophy may only be an opinion but many are adamant about their philosophy, live them as facts, and are irritated by those that do not believe like they do. Based on the current working definition in this book, a belief can neither be proven nor disproven. That makes my selection of fundamentals (and yours) based on beliefs. The purpose of the fundamentals is not to convince others, it is to help you make better, faster, more consistent decisions that are in alignment with who you are. And in doing so, become stronger, self-confident, and work toward inner peace.

Fundamental Assessment

We talked about four fundamentals; love, honor, believing and hope. We honed those fundamentals to some pretty specific definitions and scope. The reason for that is to make them smaller and specific enough to be useful.

The resulting definitions and scope are as follows:

love – *A willingness to prioritize another over yourself ('another' includes people in all of the various relationships, humanity as a whole, God, and animals)*

honor – *The consistent actions and commitment to your principles and beliefs*

believing – *To accept something as true, genuine, or real that cannot be proven or disproven; faith*

hope – *An actionable belief in the possibility of attaining a goal or desire*

There is no expectation that people will start to limit the use of these terms to only these definitions. The reality is that these words have many legitimate uses and some inappropriate ones and that will continue. I will continue to use them in everyday language because people use them to communicate. The reason for the honing of the definitions and scope is for personal fundamental usage. It is critical to reducing scope and clarifying your understanding of the fundamentals in order to achieve the benefits.

While working through the four fundamentals we acknowledged not only the relationship between fundamentals but also the dependency between them in many cases. Some of the initial ideas of potential fundamentals could not be addressed without having multiple fundamentals. You will see more of those in the next part of this book.

The Fabric

I also referred to the fabric that is *you*; so let's talk about the fabric a little more. The fabric in its most simplistic form is the intersection of all of the fundamentals. Love certainly intersects with itself and it is also likely that love will intersect with other fundamentals. Love has a higher propensity to be tied with believing. Hope can also be closely related to love but typically in a dependency role rather than a partner role; because you love, you can have hope. That does not mean that if you love, you will have hope. Honor stands as both a complement and a challenger to all of the other fundamentals which can seem conflicting, but more often will likely be affirming.

Referencing Aristotle, "the whole is greater than the sum of its parts." [13] Of course that is not true mathematically, but I believe it to be true philosophically. The whole (the fabric) makes something not only bigger than the fundamentals but makes something new. In fact

Part 1: The Fundamentals

it can make many new things depending on how the fabric is used and for what function.

If you take the literal representation of a fabric and represent the fundamentals as threads, an analogy could look like the following. Each thread might be of a different color and different weight or texture and because of that, you can use them for different things. You can sew with thread and tie things with thread and you can braid threads to make them stronger. If you weave the threads into a fabric, you now have something that you can use for cleaning up a mess or making clothes that both protect you and define a style of who you are. These uses of a fabric would be very difficult to do with a thread or even multiple threads. The fabric provides much more breadth and greater flexibility than any thread possibly could. We have spent most of the time so far on the individual fundamentals because without thread, you can't have fabric. If you understand what the fabric is made of, you have a better idea of how to use it and how to care for it. This is the concept of the fundamentals of life.

Honor   Hope

Love

Believing

The fabric is *you* because it contains the fundamentals of why you make the decisions that you do. It is flexible enough to be woven into the fabric that it needs to be. It is conscious enough to be aware of its surroundings and adapt. And it is always looking to clarify itself. Does it seem odd to talk about the fabric as being conscious? Remember the fabric is *you*.

Outside of Fundamentals

Four fundamentals of life? That's all there is? Hardly! The fundamentals are the *foundation* to everything that we do and everything that we are. They are not everything. There are all of the internal and external influencers that both contribute to and detract from your ability to make decisions. The external forces include general information, situational context to a decision, and both positive and negative influences. Internal contributors include your knowledge from previous experiences, your principles, your patterns and your emotional core.

All fundamentals are actionable rather than reactionary. They are core to living and making decisions. These fundamentals exist in a positive state of mind and as a method to reduce life's complexities to common denominators. While it does help to reduce complexities, it does not always make things completely clear. Using the fundamentals and their occasional challenges in interaction with each other can force us into a level of prioritization. If you are a pre-planned purest in your execution, you may think that you have ordered all of the priorities of the fundamentals and removed the challenge of situational prioritization. I don't know anyone who has done this and I would not suggest trying. As we have discussed, circumstances and context can always have a big impact on your priorities.

It is obvious that context, perspectives, and things that happen in life will matter. Very difficult decisions will need to be made, but knowing that you are talking about love rather than about finances or objects or even other emotions, gets the focus where it belongs. You will maybe notice that money is not one of the fundamentals and yet so much effort, discussion, and arguments end up being about that rather than what it really is about. This also brings into the discussion the idea of what motivates people. This and other operational concepts of life is what will be discussed in the rest of this book. Other than money, two very big motivators are power and success. Success is such a subjective word that it is meaningless and yet people chase their own concept of it. Motivation is good and goals are good and, at some point, most people reach a common understanding of what their motivations need to be or should have been. Remember the discussion on the origins of motivators and goals.

I want to make clear as well that I realize that the perspective of fundamentals that is being portrayed is on the rosy side of life as fundamentals should be. This does not mean that everything exists in that way by any means, or that there are not more factors in life than these four fundamentals. There are many specific facts of life that have not been mentioned. In order to make this more realistic, one very large category should be briefly mentioned. That category is pain. Whether the pain is physical or emotional, pain is a fact of life that requires some fundamentals to address. This very broad category of pain includes fear, which causes emotional and potentially physical pain. Some people's lives become consumed with pain and others will encounter pain in what seem to be random occurrences over which they would seem to have no control. The trigger of the pain is often something over which you have no control. The only influence you have is your reaction to the trigger. Finding a way to address pain will likely require your entire fabric.

Out of Your Control

We have discussed the various impacts of your fundamentals, principles, and external information on your decisions. Many of those are out of your control but contribute to the context of a situation and your ultimate decision. Many of those external out of your control factors are noise to the decision but may occasionally have impact. We have also discussed that despite those factors, there are patterns that can be identified or created to both reduce noise as well as address the unexpected.

The other aspects of impacts out of your control are the ones that happen *after* a decision. These are the ones we will discuss now.

This can be a very difficult situation that can result in blaming yourself for a result that is not as expected. This is another place where there is a line that will need to be defined by your fundamentals and principles. The line should be as close to a direct cause and effect as possible.

Let's say you purchased a plane ticket for a friend and in doing so you decided on the airline and flight time that would save the most money. That flight had a problem and crashed. You could blame yourself because if you had selected a different flight your friend would not have been in a plane that crashed. Unless you sabotaged the plane or hired someone to do it, this result has absolutely no direct cause and effect relationship with your decision. The learning from this should not be to tune your fundamentals or adjust your decisions, it should be further validation that you cannot control everything related to your decisions and help you confirm the position of your line.

Asking yourself if there was anything else you could have done might be a reasonable self-assessment question. The answer will always be you *could have* done something *different*. Different does not imply *better*. The purpose of your fundamentals and this whole process is to make decisions that are *you*; in that sense you could not have done anything else and still be you. You make decisions with the information that you have at the time. As in the example, you did not know what was going to happen to the plane or you would have selected a different flight but you clearly did not and could not have known. Asking yourself about what else could have been done often leads to very negative thoughts about yourself, including blame, self-doubt, and shame.

Part 1: The Fundamentals

Patterns

The fabric is flexible and can adapt to changing context but patterns will still evolve and be very useful. Patterns are largely driven by principles, priorities, and previous experience. They can also be *discovered* by repeated behaviors.

Even within love, the various people that you love can potentially end up in conflict as we have discussed. In the most basic sense, what if a decision related to one person has even the potential of a negative impact on another that you love? Even if the priority is clear between two people, what if it is positive for one and negative for many? When you consider the relationships across the fundamentals, it can aid in providing clarity. The more you understand your mindset and priorities, the more repeatable the decisions will be and the more resolved and comfortable you will be.

It is probably best to give you an idea of a pattern. We have talked about love a lot and the various subjects of love. Let's draw an imaginary line around your children and say that there are decisions specific to them that can eliminate noise and identify a pattern. When it comes to the health of your children, what will you not do to help your children? Is money an issue? How much money would you give up to give your children health? Let's say you have no dollar limit, even if it risks losing your house. Would you give up time? Let's say you would give up all of your time, even to the point of losing your job. I could go on but the point is that once you know where love in these situations lies, there is a pattern that can remove all other noise. Examples of noise in this situation might be people telling you that you cannot lose your job or the bank telling you that they are going to foreclose; it could even be something more minor such as someone looking at you like they don't approve of what you are doing because they don't understand why. They may think you are ignoring your responsibilities or your friends, etc.

Noise! Taking the noise out not only reduces the complexity, it allows for more time to be spent on the *important* things.

More patterns will continue to evolve as you make your fundamentals functional and put the circle of fundamentals in motion.

The Circle of Fundamentals

What is the circle? The circle is the process, the journey, and the continual evolution of yourself. This is not the *circle of life* as in *life and death*. This is within your life. The creation and realization of your fundamentals, the use of the fundamentals, the learning, the growth, the heightened awareness, the reassessment, the confidence, the consistency, the satisfaction, the calm and the inner peace. As with a circle, there is no end to the journey. That is not a burden; it is a joy. The circle might be depicted as a line because the journey has some cumulative aspects as in a linear process. That linear concept will be discussed more in the chapter on learning. The general idea is that each time you pass a point in the circle, it has the opportunity to be bigger and better. Sometimes you have to experience one thing before you can recognize another.

Without the concept of the circle, people would become fixed in their ideas including their principles, priorities, and the tuning of their fundamentals. You might ask how fundamentals can be of so much benefit if they are ever-changing. Some things are more likely to change than others, such as we discussed related to the concept of perception. It is not the idea that your fundamentals will change or the concept of right and wrong will change, but as you probably noticed the process of honing the definitions and scope of fundamentals was not exactly straightforward and had iterations. Once fundamentals are found, it may be unlikely that entirely new fundamentals will be selected, however there is no guideline that prevents it. It is more likely that your knowledge will grow through experience and you may find a different way to think about a fundamental so that it is more useful and more consistent with fewer exceptions.

Continuously tuning and improving the fundamentals, as well as your principles, is not undermining your fundamentals or their purpose. On the contrary, it allows you to stay in touch with yourself and your knowledge. It allows you to grow. It allows you to feel the benefits. It enables turning your growing knowledge and fundamentals into wisdom. This circle will sometimes be a conscious effort but it is more something to be aware of that will happen naturally. We learn and adapt as we move through life's experiences unless we close our mind to additional information.

I already offered a caution regarding not holding *all* responsibility for impacts and outcomes. The line that was discussed regarding your responsibility vs. things out of your control applies to the circle as well. When there is clearly an identifiable cause and effect, there is reason to learn from the actions and results. There is also more information to clarify the line and understand what types of things are out of your control. This is a very important line because on one side you learn how your actions have had an impact so that you can continually improve within the circle. On the other side of the line it can release you from stress and guilt for things which you had no ability to control. Things that happen are not always someone's fault vs. you made a decision that caused something to happen. Additional input into these types of dilemmas are part of what is discussed in Part 2 of this book.

Let me take a shot at an explanation of the circle, which is actually concentric rings that feed each other:

- **Fundamentals Circle** is the process of using and maintaining your fundamentals:
  - Create
  - Tune
  - Validate and cross-check
  - Implement
    - Collection of additional information
    - Make decision
  - Assess decision
  - Loop back to the tuning of the fundamentals
- **External Influencers** press from the outside and are all around you. This ring sits outside of your fundamentals and your fundamentals are the means by which to both consume and filter out the noise. This ring contains:
  - Positive influences
  - Negative influences
  - General information
  - Context
- **Your knowledge bank** is something that has only been alluded to and sits inside and is fed by your fundamentals. In turn, it also feeds your fundamentals at the time of collecting additional information. It contains:
  - Your personal experiences
  - The history of filtered external information
  - Previous decisions
  - The patterns created from all of this
- **The inner core** sits at the center of everything and is both the benefactor of everything outside filtered through your knowledge as well as a motivator that keeps everything moving. This is the key to the perpetual motion created by

Part 1: The Fundamentals

the combination of the rings and the circle of fundamentals. It contains:
- Self-worth
- Confidence
- Principles
- Inner peace

The visual representation of that looks like this:

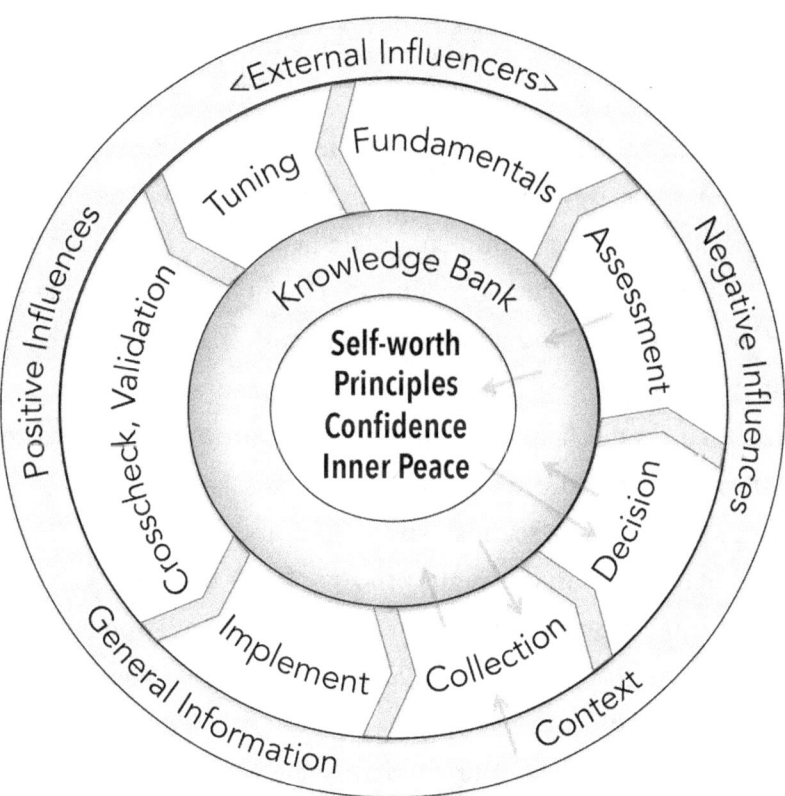

I want to explain a little more about the perpetual motion and growing effectiveness of the circle. While the fundamentals continue through their circle, the amount of knowledge and your inner core make the circle turn faster, more accurately, and with more confidence, which in turn gives more growth to the knowledge and inner core. That relationship and process is key to the effectiveness of the process. In addition, if you look at the diagram, consider that the impact (size) of the knowledge ring and the inner core will increase over time. Where is the room made for their growth? They will make your fundamentals more efficient but not shrink them. What will shrink to make room for their growth are the negative external influencers. These are not processes that you will need to think about.

Make Your Own

As stated in the beginning, fundamentals are who you are which means that everybody has to own their own fundamentals. That does not mean that everyone's fundamentals have to be different. It does mean that they *might* be and it almost certainly means that the results based on context, additional information, and previous experience will be different. This is not a method that makes everyone the same; it is a method that should help you be more consistent in executing who you are. If you know who you are, the circle begins.

The process of creating and beginning to execute on your fundamentals is not an overnight process. It is a discovery and analysis process during which you will find new things about yourself. Many things may not be new but you have just not thought about them in the context of *whys*.

The idea of creating your fundamentals was mentioned but since then I have intentionally portrayed the fundamentals as *the* fundamentals rather than *my* fundamentals. I needed to be, and wanted you to be, absorbed in the process of working through the details of finding and honing them. I also asked that you read the rest of this book before deciding to start from scratch in this process. It may very well be that you can use much of what has been outlined once you understand more about the underlying reasoning, philosophy and motivation. You are still encouraged to keep reading.

As a refresher, the steps in the process were generally:
1. Write down ideas of the things that you believe are the reasons that you make decisions
2. Vet those ideas for meeting the criteria for a fundamental such as they answer *why* you do or decide what you do
3. Reduce the list, as it is likely to be pretty long, to the lowest common denominators trying to stay under 6
4. Verify that the resulting list of fundamentals covers all of your initial ideas
5. Tune the fundamentals by using a dictionary, cross-checking with other fundamentals for conflicts or overlaps
6. Reduce scope, again tuning the definition, to filter out all but the *important* aspects
7. Begin the continuous improvement process in the circle

This is the general outline of the process used in this book. It is not an absolute checklist and you may find other steps that are useful to you, but it is a good starting point. Another potential starting point would be to start with these fundamentals and let the process of the circle make modifications as necessary. Again, this is not a one and done adventure.

The next part of this book will provide more insight into more details of the underpinnings of the fundamentals that were selected, other factors that influenced the selections, and realities of life that either support or will obstruct the use of fundamentals.

Moving Forward

We make decisions and our decisions and subsequent actions speak louder about who we are than our words. Some may misperceive the last statement of "speak louder about who we are". Who does that speak to and how do we know? It speaks to yourself because you are the one that knows not only your actions, but also your motivations, goals, and who you are. Others will *feel* your actions ring true to them, especially over time, but that might not be the initial reaction for many. Our consistency with what we *know* is all that we ultimately have in this regard. The trap for many lies in basing your perceptions on others' perceptions or, even more complex, on your perception of others' perceptions.

Many people would much rather see and hear what they want, even if they know it is a lie, rather than see and hear truth and honesty. It is human nature to want to feel validation; so many are willing to accept a perception that they could know is not true if they looked. Yes, surprise, people lie to themselves. My point in this is not to get bogged down in a behavior of humanity; it is to provide you with a caution not to look to others to tell you who you are or how your actions are aligning with who you are.

Do you ever look at people in positions of power, whether it is in private companies or in government and wonder how they got there? It is a good possibility that this premise is how it happened; they are willing to tell people what they want to hear rather than the truth of who they are. I don't want this caution to seem negative but I do not want to give you the false perception that identifying and living your life based on your fundamentals will be easy, or that everyone will instantly appreciate you for it. It is a journey that is not recognized by the superficial judgment of others and living your life with a mask is not a healthy or peaceful place to be.

Part 1: The Fundamentals

Part 2 of this book will look at the operational implementation of fundamentals, some of the initial ideas for fundamentals, aspects of life that *happen*, and considerations for understanding yourself and others. Understanding yourself and others is critical to the understanding, validation, implementation of your fundamentals, and your resulting decisions.

PART 2
Life's Realities

Supporting and Inhibiting Realities of Life

Chapter 2-1
IMPLEMENTATION AND LIFE'S REALITIES

I titled this part of the book *Life's Realities* because the intent is to bring real life into the discussion of fundamentals. Four fundamentals and life is good and everything is clear? Maybe you can close the book and move on? You could but please don't. As important as fundamentals are to life, there is more to discuss. The fundamentals focused on the lowest common denominators (fundamentals) used to make the *important* decisions. We then added the concept of external influencers, patterns, your inner core, and how they are related to each other. What is left?

There are details included in the initial ideas for fundamentals. There are also supporting functions to the fundamentals as well as aspects of life that impact the implementation of the fundamentals (positive and negative influences). This part of the book provides real examples of both of these.

Most of the chapters in this book have a relationship to other chapters but you will find that the chapters are not grouped in categories or listed in a specific order. I had to take a shot at the order but there is so much that can be related and intertwined across these topics that there is not a specific sequence that would be "right". Learning can be linear, as in you cannot learn or observe something before first learning something else. The intersection of these examples is a matrix just like fundamentals and life itself; any order selected will miss a connection. Reading them in a different order would likely provide a different experience, so regardless of the order, it is not the *only* order that makes sense.

As stated, the purpose of these chapters is to provide real-life examples that have both positive and negative impacts on the fundamental circle.

Some chapters in this part of the book may seem like they are negative by looking at the titles of the chapters. While there are chapters that reflect information and growth in their titles, even the negatives offer an opportunity for growth. Recognition of the world's realities does not mean that we become what we acknowledge.

There is more included in the chapters than examples. Some of the chapters present aspects of both implementing and tuning the fundamentals and the chapter on learning is one of them. Learning is used to tune our fundamentals and how we learn is impacted by the fundamentals (another impact of the circle). This is life. Everything is intertwined and has the opportunity to impact another, which can impact another, and so on. The sequence can be different each time.

Other potential benefits from these chapters might be to provide more insight into why these four fundamentals were selected, as there are common themes throughout. It may also spur thoughts of your own as you look at creating or validating your own fundamentals.

As stated, some of these realities and functions of life support the fundamentals. The honing and tuning process of fundamentals alone requires the ability to distinguish facts from perceptions as well as the ability to learn and apply what has been learned. Honor referred to principles, integrity, and respect. These topics and more are explored in greater detail.

As you read through this part of the book, you may see things that you agree with and things that you disagree with. You may learn and you may be spurred to more personal evaluation, more research, or more self-assessment. In the end, these examples of life's realities should bring you closer to your fundamentals. The point of this is not to control your thoughts but offer information as well as my perceptions and beliefs for you to consider. When you have more substance behind your fundamentals, you are much more likely to be confident in them and utilize them. You are much more likely to be at peace with your life and your decisions. That is a very powerful state of mind.

Some of these chapters will make a direct reference to one or more fundamentals, while some may not mention them at all. You may draw your own relationships based on your specific experiences or form alternate positions on the topics.

The way that they tie to fundamentals is specific and personal to you and what makes you who you are. Recognizing how you tie them and sharing that with others can help you and others and it is under that premise that I will share some of mine.

There are some very big topics covered in these short chapters. Each of these chapters could be a book unto themselves and there are likely many books on each topic. There is plenty of room for you to personally expand on each of them.

Chapter 2-2
EVERYTHING IS RELATIVE

It was stated that each of these chapters could be and probably are books of their own. This chapter is one that I have actually considered writing a book about. It has been part of me for a very long time and is part of most everything that I do, think, or say. That being said, it would be very ironic and even hypocritical of me if I did not recognize something new that I discovered while writing this book. That discovery emphasizes the point of relativity but also requires that my position on this statement be clarified.

This need for clarity is driven by the philosophy summary that covered Relativism. When I say, "everything is relative," it does not mean what it would mean within Relativism as a philosophy. That could result in someone misunderstanding my statement. I still know what it means to me, but the primary purpose for me noting that everything is relative is that it is relative to a person. Part of the Relativism philosophy concludes that there is no "right", there is no "truth", and nothing stands on its own. I do not believe that and, therefore, do not want my statement to potentially imply to some that I do. The two primary situations where this statement applies are when communicating with another person or when applying adjectives to your memory for your own use. Read on through this chapter and you will see what I mean.

There are so many aspects of relativity and it comes up every day for me. A key point of this is the first word, EVERYTHING. It might be safer and more accurate to state that everything *can be* relative. Many people might tend to think of this only applying to adjectives and adverbs such as big or cheap or slow but there are much deeper implications because we are human. Our perception, our experiences, and our current state of mind impact how we subconsciously process the relativity or context of everything. It applies to everything that is not *absolute*. Absolute being something that can only have one interpretation. Let's first look at the more straightforward relativity examples, which are complex enough. They are not so complex to talk about but very difficult to execute.

Adjectives and Adverbs

Slow, rich, cheap and small are basic examples but every adjective and adverb is subject to relativity. One of the major reasons that this is important is that it significantly impacts communication and understanding.

Using slow as an example, if someone says "It was slow", what does that create in your head? Did you interject what *it* was? Did you instantly ask yourself what *it* was? Slow implies speed. If you use a turtle or an animal or a person or a car or a plane, how does that change your perception of slow? Speed has a value. Let's use miles per hour as that measurement. How many miles per hour is a slow turtle vs. a slow car? This is merely giving the context of the associated noun.

Using car as the noun, if I am a NASCAR fan, or driver, or have something that triggers that as a context for me, then 80 mph is probably very slow; whereas if you are talking about normal city driving, 80 mph is very fast. 80 mph would be an example of an absolute.

Adding qualifiers such as "compared to" is not usually part of most people's conversational language, so the listener implies the context and the context is then very often out of sync with the intention.

Absolute values such as 20 mph are facts that allow each person to imply their own context and create their own subconscious adjectives and adverbs. While this is factual and more precise communication, it is probably not the most common because it would not be good storytelling. While using slow rather than 20 mph puts some context in the conversation, the context is only known to the presenter unless it is further explained. Most people will not assume that an explanation is needed because their context is all they know and it is a natural assumption that all people have the same context.

Use of relativity as a tool of manipulation is also a reality. The adjectives such as slow are not facts, so they carry little accountability and they can certainly be abused. How often when someone claims that someone is mean, or dirty, or crabby is the term of "in my opinion", "because", or "compared to" used in the statement? Qualifiers are almost never used unless it is a purely legal connotation where libel or defamation might be charged. If someone states that someone is mean and the listener either wants to believe it, or has no reason or desire to challenge it or clarify it, it is taken as corroboration of fact.

The purpose of this topic is not to tell you that you need to personally investigate everything that you hear, but rather to be aware of the relativity of statements and the impact that they present in conclusions related to perceptions. The more you are aware of these and turn these into patterns, the more useful the statements become and the more you are able to both understand as well as convey a message.

I used some exaggerated examples such as NASCAR and city driving for speed, but the real risk in normal daily living is much more subtle than that. People can generally understand the extremes but the personal perceptions and context often get glossed over by assumptions that everyone is on the same page because everybody knew the context of the conversation. What everybody does not have are the same experiences and same background in order to draw the same conclusions.

Everything Else

Adjectives and adverbs are probably the most prevalent and easiest concept to understand, not that it is easy to keep in your thought process. Nouns are much more complex. Let's use dad as a first example of a noun that has deeper meaning and implications. It is a fact that dad is the biological male that created a child. It is also not limited to that. Adopted parents can be a very real mom and dad to a child. When you say dad, what is associated with the listener? A good relationship or a horrible relationship? We could go back to cars and with no other context, the person may relate to their car or a dream car or who knows what car. Depending on the story, it may or may not make a difference.

Another example is the relativity of images. You can believe what you see, right? I took a picture of some rocks that were stacked and based on the relative perspective of the things around them, you would think that they are massive, maybe 20-30 feet across. Just then, when I said massive, did you think bigger than 20-30 feet? My perspective of massive (and I let that language flow) was based on the fact that I know the rocks are actually 2-3 inches. They normally sit with a background of my bedroom dresser. So, things are relative to your perception and history with the item but also with their current context. How do you get to the facts of the information when it is all contextually manipulated and, in some cases, intentionally manipulated? You are cautious and you ask questions.

The Importance of Relativity

The importance of relativity lies primarily in two situations. The most obvious from the examples is communication. This one in itself is big enough to try to always keep in mind. Communication, or more accurately miscommunication can lead to total disconnects, bad feelings, failed objectives and even war. When you combine the unintentional lack of context with assumptions, manipulation, and the occasional lies, how is anyone supposed to know the truth or gain trust?

Most people don't think of this concept in their daily lives and most of those that do still find a way to manage their lives and find trust in some people. It is, however, a different approach that may seem insurmountable at first. The first and biggest step is to realize that relativity matters and each person has their own perspective of the meaning of words. There is a saying regarding assumptions that I don't think I need to repeat, but this concept of relativity is the primary reason for the saying.

Other than communication with others, the scenario that can be very impactful to your life is internal. The process of clarification of the context is the same, but there is no communication with others (yet). It is the way that you store the memory. Things that are stored without context become altered facts over time in your memory.

Think about being a child and storing the memory of your grandparent being very old. When you are sixty and recall your memories of your grandparent as being old, you may not think about them as actually being ten years younger than you are right now. This one is probably too easy and some may actually adjust their memories over time or write off the memory to being a "child". Let's use another example of putting a label on someone as a liar, a thief, or a "bad" person. Those labels can last in your memory for a very long time and in some cases the context of the label can never be recalled. Think about a time when you experienced the worst pain you have ever felt until you felt something that was worse. How do you know that the more recent one was worse if you simply recorded the previous example as the worst? You clearly have other memories that allow you to compare something other than the label of worst. That label is only *moveable* because of other memories. It is helpful to keep that concept in mind with other labels.

In clarifying my statement of "everything is relative", I could add the condition in explaining that statement to be constrained to *when communicating with others or when putting labels on memories*. I will likely not add those conditions again in this book or every time that I speak, but I will certainly keep in mind the fact that there are people that believe in Relativism as a philosophy and could misunderstand the meaning of my statement. Another way of putting that is to say that *everything can be relative*, where Relativism would say everything *must be* relative. The importance of relativity will continue to show its relevance throughout this book and every place you look once you recognize its pervasive existence.

Chapter 2-3
LEARNING

Learning is very important to the fundamental circle. It is an opportunity that presents itself prior to, during, and after all decisions. It is an essential part of tuning and validating our fundamentals as well as building knowledge from external influencers and experience.

Learning is not just something that happens in school or formal coursework. Learning is something that happens continually with people that are not closed to the world and accept that they don't know everything. I see too many people that seem to have shut down any possibility of learning and have replaced it with a superficial recognition of others' knowledge only for the purpose of benefiting from the recognition rather than for the opportunity to learn.

Let's address the way that we learn and the way that we evolve with age. This topic like so many others, by the nature of a life, will cross over into other topics. In addition, by the continual process of learning, the topic itself will evolve.

Entering into a euphoric spiral: The sooner we learn, the more time we have to utilize that knowledge. The more time we have to utilize that knowledge, the better off we are. The better off we are, the better off the world is.

This obviously assumes that people use knowledge for good, which if you have read anything else from me you understand that I don't believe that they always do. I do, however, believe that people thinking for themselves with true knowledge will result in the "bad people" having less ability to manipulate others which occasionally happens en masse. Some people are more than happy to follow based on emotions and feelings with no knowledge.

Later in this book, just like later in life, the *evolution of knowledge* will be addressed. It would *seem* that facts are truths and facts are not likely to change, but perceptions do change and perceptions are the vast majority of our operational facts.

Listening

So how do people learn? Why do some people learn and others don't or at least take much longer to learn? A key component of learning that many fail at is listening. There is a quote that is believed to be from Mark Twain that states, "It ain't what you don't know that gets you in trouble. It's what you know for sure that just ain't so." [14] How can anybody possibly learn if they know everything? How do you keep your mind open for learning? I believe that it is important for learning to be a perpetual state of mind.

Understanding the context is a critical component of learning that has an impact on how you listen. As an example, you have probably heard the Ben Franklin quote, "in this world nothing can be said to be certain, except death and taxes." [15] The latter is not true because some have certainly proven that not everyone pays taxes. I do not believe that death is the *only* certainty but the other certainties that I believe in are either:

- point in time observations
- somewhat vague so that they allow for variations
- come with qualifiers

The *qualifiers* and the *point-in-time observations* are a type of context. Examples of qualified *certainties* include things such as it is illegal to take a life and even 2+2 = 4. The first might make you instantly think about the qualifiers, especially in the context of me stating that these are qualified certainties. Take this statement out of this context and put it in another such as after a mass murder, or after a terror attack, a home invasion, war or abortion and the conversation and thought processes my take a very different path.

When you are in a particular context, it does not mean that the other person is in that same context. This can be due to many different reasons, not the least of which is just plain failure to clarify the context. As I said, the taking of a life is something that for many would bring an instant thought on contexts that might change the answer. This might not be as true for 2+2; but nonetheless, it is possible to change the context and the answer. We are probably all used to base 10 and our numeric system but there is such a thing as base 2, base 3 and so on. In base three only 0s,1s and 2s exist, so 2+2 cannot equal 4. I am not suggesting that you need to qualify every numeric statement with base 10; it is to make the point that variation of context can apply in ways that you might not think.

All of this rambling on death, taxes, killing and math is to make the point that the only way to be productive in listening with the intent of learning is to understand the context. Many times, the only way to understand the context is to ask. Some may think you are stupid for asking, but that is their issue and should not prevent you from learning.

This is starting to cross over, as many topics will, into another initial fundamental idea that will come up later, respect. In order to learn you listen, and in order to be motivated to listen you must respect that there is something to be learned from others. I would even say that there is something to be learned from everyone. At one point in my life, I worked with mentally handicapped children and adults with estimated IQs under 50 and I learned a lot from them. You have to be willing. In their context, they addressed situations to absolutely ingenious resolution.

If you listen to *all* that there is to offer, does it not get in the way of being decisive or self-confident? It seems that some believe that they are completely infallible and therefore they can be rude in the process. There are times when decisions need to be made and not everybody's input can be heard but those situations are probably the exception. You would likely not find anyone that I have worked with that would not say that I am decisive, provide direction and have a strong opinion on almost everything. A key word here is opinion. If you operate from the fact that you have an opinion rather than the opinion that you have all of the facts, you can listen *and* be decisive.

Summarizing so far:
1. You listen to learn
2. You respect input from others
3. You understand that everyone's context may be different and make the effort to clarify
4. You are open to your thoughts being opinions that may be changed based on information provided by others

With this process, it seems to me that some may take this as being an academic touchy-feely approach to listening. It is not! This is not suggesting that you write these down and go through them whenever you have a conversation. This is also not suggesting that you have to accept everything that you hear from others; remember the concept of noise. These are some of the principles by which I try to live. They are part of my everyday life and part of my inner core.

Understanding

Learning is *not* memorization. The concept of memorization starts early in school, at least it did for me. Certainly, remembering information is of value but it doesn't mean that you understand anything other than there is a correlation between two pieces of information such as a question and an answer or a date and an event. The memory of just these things is useful as long as all you need to know is the relationship between these items.

I also want to bring up behavioral conditioning at this point which is often referred to as learning. Learned behaviors are different than conditioned behaviors. This section is about understanding because that type of learning is the type that can grow into knowledge and wisdom and be used to create patterns. Conditioned behavior is a cause and effect response like Pavlov's dog. I spent many years studying behavior management, writing, and executing plans. It is a very powerful tool if you want to manipulate a reactionary response to a trigger. It is used a lot today in marketing, politics, "education", and by many that want you to behave in a certain way. I am not going to spend any more time on this but I wanted to share that I do not believe behavioral conditioning to be learning, or at least of a type that is useful for the purpose of this book other than to be aware that it exists.

Understanding *why* allows for the use of the information in many different applications. Some might say that it is the difference between smart and wise; knowledge and wisdom are discussed in another chapter. Memorization provides nothing more to me than the ability to remember. When you are able to apply the knowledge that you have gained outside of the circumstances under which it was acquired, you have entered the *learning zone*.

Discovering Patterns

Observing patterns is where the real essence of learning comes into play. Patterns are the keys to knowledge and wisdom. You can find correlation of two or more things that are seemingly unrelated but share the same pattern or find patterns that are of a high enough level to be reusable elsewhere. This is the same concept as finding patterns of fundamental usage for decisions; in fact, patterns for decisions are a subset of learning patterns in general.

Here are a few simple examples:
- You throw a rock in the water and it sinks. You throw a brick in the water and it sinks. You throw a ball in the water and it floats. You could go on putting things in the water and remember whether each one floats or sinks or you can find the pattern that anything heavier than water sinks. I know, it is physics but someone had to find the pattern.
- You could yell for your friend John in the theater and people tell you to sit down and shut up. It must be because they don't like John, right? If you yell again, you might find a pattern regardless of what you yell (unless you yell John again).

These are very simple and maybe silly examples but everybody has the opportunity to find their own. I have found many that may only work for me while others might be universal and some of the patterns that I have found are embedded throughout this book.

Part 2: Life's Realities

Fundamental Process (the Circle) and Learning

Learning is not only related to the fundamental circle, it is a requirement for the circle to reach a perpetual state. Yes, you need to learn, listen, and understand. In order to turn that into knowledge, not to undermine the openness required to learn, you must apply previous knowledge and patterns in order to ascertain what is new information vs. the same information with a new coat of paint. I have to bring this up because there is a lot of time wasted on new coats of paint presenting themselves as new ideas. This is just more noise when it comes to defining patterns.

Without digging too far into why people will claim old ideas as new ones, it is reasonable to assume that either they were unaware of the previous "discovery" or they are self-serving in their intent to "steal" an existing idea. Regardless, for our own benefit, it is important to recognize the difference between new information and things that are just new labels or rhetoric.

Whether it be in a business, technical, or social environment, there is an overabundance of new terms that are nothing more than new labels stuck on old ideas. From the standpoint of your fundamentals and your decisions, this new label is nothing more than clutter and is most beneficial to discard. The only reason to even recognize it is for communication with others. If others are using the new terms, you may have better communication skills if you can translate the new terms in your head. These terms are often in the category of "buzzwords" which are terms that people like to use but most of the time, have nothing new to offer.

I could offer some buzzword examples but my concern is that they would be outdated very soon. The new labels on old discoveries tend to be short lived. You likley have examples from your line of work or daily activities. One of my previous lines of work was related to data management and data integration. Anybody with a new product related to those activities would tend to invent new labels to make their product sound like a new discovery. Data integration is moving data and regardless of what label or what tool, it is still moving data. Storing data is storing data regardless of a floppy disk, a tape, a hard drive, or the cloud. They store data. Sure the technology and physical characteristics are different, but so many make it sound like storing data is new. As I said, the new labels move so fast but hopefully you get the picture. Again, the reason that is important, is that if you are creating patterns that are related to the underlying function or purpose (such as data storage), you need to be able to put them all together for the most robust and accurate pattern that uses all of the information as well as tosses any redundant information.

I have used the term linear learning but that may give a false impression. It simply means that you need to learn some things before you can learn other things. You obviously cannot learn everything all at once. It may be that you can't understand some things at all until you learn something else, or it may be that you understand them in a different or more complete way than you possibly could have without the previous information. Can you imagine a sentence without words or math without numbers? Classes are taught in a sequence for a reason but some things are not that regimented, such as life. You experience them in the order that they happen. Circling back on things that you think you know, once you know something else, can present lots of new opportunities for learning.

A concept may be given to you or you may see or read something and think you have some understanding, or you might just brush it off because it doesn't seem that relevant or important. Later when you see it, you say to yourself, "Oh, that's what it means". Learning, just like life, is a matrix and every intersection has new opportunities.

Chapter 2-4
COMMUNICATION

Communication has so many ties. It is a major part of learning, teaching, relationships, and pretty much anything that is not internal processing. It is deeply dependent upon understanding relativity. There are many types of communication. Some are verbal, some are images, some are written words, and there are more. Images leave the interpretation entirely to the viewer; written words are very susceptible to relative interpretation of the words. I am going to look at the communication that allows for interaction because it is the most effective and allows for the communicator as well as the listener to have some responsibility for the outcome. This might be better referred to as conversation rather than communication. I am going to leave it as communication because there are things that the listener should be aware of and things they can do even if they cannot speak with the communicator. This chapter will focus on the two sides of the communication equation.

The Communicator

As the communicator, you are going to share something with someone. You hopefully have a purpose in this sharing other than a need to hear yourself talk. You may want someone to understand something that you think they do not; you are playing the educator. You may be explaining something for which you want their feedback; you are playing the student. You may be sharing your opinion or facts and it is highly likely that you want or even need them to understand. Beyond that purpose of understanding, it may be your desire for them to align with and support what you are saying. It may be that you need their help so you want them to fully understand in order to offer you the most effective help.

This is not going to be a marketing session, but it is extremely important that you understand your audience. An audience of one is still an audience. You are lost as a communicator if they don't listen. You first need to understand them well enough to know what it will take for them to listen. Are they interested in what you are saying and if not, what can you say that is related to something they are interested in? Some would refer to this as spin but I would not take it that far; it is not altering or manipulating the facts but adding a perspective that is of interest. The facts and integrity of your statements are extremely important and need to stay intact. You need to stay aligned with your fundamentals and principles.

Once you have people listening, the aspects of perspective, fact, and relativity become the critical factors. As we have already discussed, the adjectives, adverbs and even nouns will have different meanings to different people which makes communicating the context of the statements critical; making them statements that are measurable and quantifiable arguments. If you have been specific in the context, it still does not mean the person you are communicating with will understand the meaning of what you are saying. This is where it is going to fall on the receiver. Some receivers are just going to hear what they want to hear regardless of what you say. It shouldn't stop you from trying to preserve your own personal integrity, hopes, and beliefs. However, *winning* them *all* is not likely and disappointments will occur.

The Receiver

This is in direct alignment with learning. This should potentially be labeled as the listener but a real part of communication is understanding that the receiver may not be listening. If there is an attempt to communicate but failure to listen, for whatever reason, it is a failed communication. In this case, the accountability is not just with the receiver, it lies with both the receiver *and* the communicator. Maybe the communicator is just plain boring or maybe the receiver is so tired they are falling asleep, or one of thousands of other reasons that someone may not listen.

Both sides are impacted but it is probably more likely that the receiver's mood is a factor in the communication. They may not be in the mood to listen; they may have a preconceived idea of what is going to be said because of the situation or perception of the person speaking. Can you, as the receiver, separate yourself from preconceived notions of the person or topic long enough to listen and learn? Many cannot. This again goes back to the practice of learning and the balance between confidence, arrogance, and humility.

Nobody is going to be able to start with an absolute clean slate. We all carry our perceptions and experiences that will influence what we hear. This influence is not the blatant preconceived ideas and conclusions about the person or topic, it is the relative influence of the words that are used. When the person communicating said "small", what did they mean or how did you interpret it? Those types of relative qualifications will have a significant impact on your conclusions. Even if you have taken the topic's preconceived conclusions out, you owe it to yourself to understand the context. While the communicator should be providing the context and not leaving the interpretation open, you should ask questions of context if it has not been made clear.

Communication is a skill. It takes practice. We only touched on the basic concept of understanding and being understood. I will note my opinion that social media has only made it that much more difficult. While the access is so easy, the clarity gets lost and misunderstandings are prevalent.

Chapter 2-5
PERCEPTION VS. FACTS

It is getting harder and harder to distinguish between the two and in some circumstances it doesn't matter. That seems wrong! The truth doesn't matter? To clarify, from a standpoint of truth it matters very much, but from the aspect of the impact, reaction, and outcomes, too often there is no difference. A person's perception is most often what they treat as fact. It is certainly possible that the open-minded and self-aware individual will realize that it is a perception rather than a fact, but in reality that should not be expected of others and the most advisable operating mode should be to assume that another person's fact is actually their perception.

How to Tell the Difference

When it comes to facts, be aware of terms such as: I believe, I heard, I think, I bet, they will, because, and personality labels. These terms indicate that conclusions have been drawn by that person based on experience, some form of evidence, or even less; these are perceptions. Explicit terms like I said, she said, I did, and it was, *might* be facts. It can be a fact that she said something; if you add I heard that she said or she said *because*, it falls back to a perception. There can be no fact in someone else's *why*. Why something happened can only be offered as a "potential" fact from the person that owns the reason that they themselves did something. Only in that circumstance is it *potentially* a fact and even then, it might not be. Any other person (someone else) making a statement of why something happened is always perception.

These are indicators but the majority of the time these obvious indicators of perceptions are not present and information is provided as though it was fact. It is even a reasonable indicator of perception or manipulation when someone says "everybody knows" or "the fact is".

In determining the best description of the difference between fact and perception, you could say that one is true and one *might* be true. The criterion for facts is a pretty high bar. Facts are not statements of anything in the future. In a timeline they move from present backward. Time constraints can be difficult but even facts are constrained by time. An easy example is that when I was in school, it was a fact that there were 9 planets in our solar system and Pluto was one of them. This was a scientific *fact*. It is no longer a fact today. That object referred to as a planet didn't go anywhere; it is just no longer a planet and that is a fact (today).

There are many more subtle examples of time constraints such as stating what the weather is, what time it is, how you feel, and what you are eating to name a few. These are statements that most would assume the time constraint and would not hold you to your answer of the weather the next day. When reporting the history of the weather statement, it could be stated as, "Yesterday it was 100 degrees at the Minneapolis airport at 2:00 PM according to the National Weather Service." That would be a fact the next day, but beyond that day would require the date as opposed to yesterday. Stating that it was hot yesterday not only is a relative term, it cannot be considered a fact because hot is subjective. This may seem like a rather silly and obvious example but the point here was how to tell the difference.

Did you personally experience the statement being made such as *you* said it, *you* heard it, or *you* did it? If so, it is a fact that you said, heard, or did it. This does not mean that you have to personally experience all facts but it does not stray too far from that. You can accept a fact that the United States declared its independence on July 4th, 1776, because there is a document that states it that is universally accepted. If the proof was a document that showed up from an anonymous source and was questioned by some, you may still choose to believe it but it would fall short of fact. Relative to the amount of information available in the world, a very, very small percentage would meet this criteria of fact.

When Does it Matter?

It matters when learning. It matters when defining patterns. It matters when making decisions. It matters when building knowledge, trust, and respect. It might be that a better question is "For whom does it matter?". To most, and most of the time, it does not matter. People will take action on perception as though it is fact. I believe, most will not even discern that there is a difference. It matters when you don't understand that there is a difference. Operating on "false" facts can be disastrous. That is not to say that we do not need to operate on perceptions. We have to choose a path based on what is available to us; however, making a decision based on a probability is different than making a decision based on fact. Perceptions are just personal calculated degrees of probability that everyone should ask *why*.

Fundamentals of Life

When it Pertains to Me

In my position at work, I have often been informed of people's perception of me in terms of my performance review. I have trouble with that concept since I don't consider it part of my job to be responsible for the perceptions of others. It is understood that some roles such as a salesman would be dependent on people's perceptions, which is why many people are not fans of salespeople. A salesperson's job, in this context, is to sell you something. In order to sell you something, they will tell you things that they believe you want to hear and will try to communicate in some way that you can trust them and what they are telling you. Much of the time, this is a perception that they want you to have rather than something that can be based on fact. That was not my job, so what could I or should I have attempted to do to change people's perceptions of me?

My role was to review and point out the validity and compliance with standards and best practices. You could compare the purpose of my role to a building or food inspector. Why would part of a performance review for these roles be based on how happy the builders or food processors were with their results? So, the people being inspected complain that the inspector was too thorough, called out specific issues, and documented all of them. The agency then reprimanded the inspector for doing what is explicitly his job. What does this have to do with perception? It is obvious that the person being inspected has a different context of reality and measurement of good than the inspector. The importance of this relates to perception vs. fact but also allows for those willing to observe the fact that there is a difference and even a conflict in the perceptions. Identifying fact is the first step. Resolving the conflicts and separation of perceptions from facts is the next.

Part 2: Life's Realities

How to Communicate the Difference

This topic largely overlaps the communication topic, in that it is the responsibility of the communicator to differentiate between fact and opinion. The communicator is responsible for gathering the information to be disseminated to others. However, the listener also has the responsibility to gather and assess the information while they are listening. I do not want to cause people to be paranoid but there is a real risk to your own knowledge base if you do not understand the difference between fact and opinion and that people will use manipulation and even lies to get what they want. Now it begins to overlap with the topic of trust.

Communicating the difference *should be*, the communicator simply calling out the difference when stating their opinion, perspective, or the source of the fact, but that cannot be relied upon. It used to be that you could rely on the communicator, when there was some reliance on newspapers or TV news reporting the *facts* and calling out when they were stepping into an opinion piece. They were careful to use words like unsubstantiated, or allegedly. That is not the case today. Even the "professionals", like doctors, will state opinion as fact. Bottom line, as the listener in a communication, take the responsibility.

Wrap Up

Whether you are the communicator or the receiver, whether the communication is visual, verbal or written, the only person that is going to be able to satisfy the criteria of *fact* is you. It is a responsibility that will impact your inner core as well as those around you. This seems like a heavy burden and it is; it also needs to be recognized that this is just another decision driven by your fundamentals and the fundamental circle and you can only decide based on what you know at the time. You will make mistakes. Mistakes are not misrepresentations or failures. Continue to learn and the facts, just like the patterns, will become more apparent.

Chapter 2-6
KNOWLEDGE

Speaking of learning from the experience of cause and effect, it is one of the biggest contributors to knowledge. I will turn to Merriam-Webster again. While there are a number of definitions listed, including an archaic definition, I will often put more weight on the first one:

knowledge: *"...the fact or condition of knowing something with familiarity gained through experience or association..."* [16]

I do not want to debate what is meant by fact in this context and it is interesting that *knowing*, which is a form of the word, is used in the definition. There I go critiquing a recognized *knowledgeable* source again. The very important aspect of this definition is how knowledge is acquired; through experience or association (learning).

Knowledge is the next step after learning that comes from the accumulated filtered information. Knowledge can be gained via books, training, and experience. I firmly believe that experience is the most impactful and that the combination of all sources is the most effective.

Books or training on their own do not hold the personal context that is applied when you experience something. Your background and the context in which you see an event and feel an associated emotion will be applied when the knowledge is applied. If it is not applied during learning, the application may be out of sync with the knowledge that was acquired without your personal context.

There is a relationship between information, learning, knowledge, intelligence and wisdom. There is a chapter that will expand on wisdom, but I first want to acknowledge that there is a long philosophical debate related to the meaning of each of these and the difference between them. I am going to share my thoughts and, at the same time, I don't particularly care what you call them. The important information is not in the label applied, but in the meaning and function of various states or stages of "knowledge".

In short, knowledge is the processed information that is acquired. Intelligence is the *ability* to learn and understand, including the ability to form patterns. The intelligent recognition or assessment of the information that identifies patterns and correlations between the pieces of information stores the information in the knowledge banks, which enables the reuse of information in more situations. Wisdom applies humanity, intent, and/or purpose to the knowledge and patterns in their application.

Knowledge is central to the rest of the terms, and the meaning and quality of the knowledge is critical. I would say that if there is not quality, it is not really knowledge. Some may believe it to be knowledge, but the vetting and appropriate qualifiers of the information are essential. There is a saying in the computer science field, at least that's where I know it from, "garbage in, garbage out". [17] This means that if you start with garbage (the information/knowledge), your results will also be garbage and carry little to no meaning or significance; it could even have a negative and detrimental impact. It is obvious therefore that the acquisition of knowledge is a critical aspect of all things that follow. This does not mean that all information needs to be vetted to the degree of being verified facts, but the context, sources, and caveats need to be captured with the information so that the full breadth of the information can remain for future use.

A simple example would be that Joe shot John. It is one thing to know this because you saw it for yourself without visual constraints and without question. It would be another important piece of information if you "know" this because Tom told you he heard that Joe shot John. You may still capture the fact that you heard this, but not in the same context as having firsthand knowledge. A variant of this could be that Joe shot John *because* he stole his car. It is far less likely for you to have firsthand knowledge of this unless Joe himself told you. This may be a compound set of assumptions that you heard John stole Joe's car, so you assume that was the reason Joe shot John. This is still information that might be worth capturing, but in a far different context. Store all the who-said and who-assumed, rather than a potentially false conclusion.

I am sorry if I offended any Joes, Johns or Toms. It just works so much better than person 1 and person 2. I also intended no offense to the male gender by selecting male names. Just kidding. I am not sorry because they are just random names with no meaning, no malicious intent and no association to a real person. If you are offended, get over it.

Now that I am over that rant, this obviously had a great deal of overlap with *perception vs. fact* because it is core to the meaning and purpose of knowledge and the resulting benefits vs. false conclusions. Knowledge, and the patterns contained within that knowledge, will build over time. The speed at which the knowledge can build will depend on your openness to learning and using your fundamentals for filtering. Regardless of the speed, it will grow over time which gets to the idea of wisdom being associated with age. Purely by longevity, there is more opportunity to acquire more knowledge. It is a shame that is missed by some that are younger. Remember, patterns are portable across situations and even across time. Building up so much knowledge over time at some point gets to the point where the challenge is less about adding more but being able to remember all that has been acquired.

As we have discussed, information, knowledge, and wisdom are key components of tuning and implementing your fundamentals and finding your inner peace.

Chapter 2-7
WISDOM

A wise man once said:
- "Rather fail with honor than succeed by fraud." [18]– Sophocles
- "True wisdom comes to each of us when we realize how little we understand about life, ourselves, and the world around us." [19] – Socrates
- "There will always be rocks in the road ahead of us. They will be stumbling blocks or stepping stones; it all depends on how you use them." [20] – Friedrich Nietzsche
- "The man who asks a question is a fool for a minute, the man who does not ask is a fool for life." [21] - Confucius

And there are so many more. It is interesting that in the research of some sample wise man quotes that the top 25 examples were all philosophers. At first, this seemed like there might be some other explanation of the sites being philosophy sites or some deep conspiracy (just kidding). There may be an answer as to why philosophers are associated with wise man quotes. Philosophy is *not* the only use of wisdom. Wisdom has real everyday implementation without going to the depths of philosophical evaluations of why things in life occur or whether they will occur. The reason is that *wisdom is defined by patterns*. Seeing patterns allows for the transport of information across multiple topics and across life. Patterns help to identify the whys.

wisdom: *the effective application of accumulated knowledge while applying humanity, intent, and/or purpose.*

The definition above is not from Merriam-Webster; it is mine. Let's compare to samples from Merriam-Webster's Dictionary:

wisdom: *"1a: ability to discern inner qualities and relationships: INSIGHT   b: good sense: JUDGMENT   c: generally accepted belief..."* [22]

The last definition may not fit but the first two are certainly in alignment with my definition. The reason I like my definition is that it fits a process for the evolution of wisdom. Information is collected, filtered, processed, and forms an accumulation of knowledge. This knowledge is reprocessed during a situation where information is needed, resulting in the application and appropriate use of the knowledge. The appropriate use is largely supported by patterns that have been identified within your knowledge bank. I am hoping that you can see the process of the fundamental circle. One might gather from this that the use of the fundamental circle results in wisdom.

You might think a chapter on wisdom would be lengthy and need to dissect deep evaluations of the current and ancient philosophers. Wisdom does not have a requirement of being verbose, so I am ending here. Wisdom can include knowing when to stop.

Part 2: Life's Realities

Chapter 2-8
PRINCIPLES

It could be argued that principles are at the core of every decision. I *believe* that they *should* be at the core of every decision. Principles sit in the inner core of the fundamental circle. Why would principles then not be more important than fundamentals or why are they not the fundamentals? That is a very reasonable question that we have touched on a bit. Principles are generally for the purpose of defining your rules around what is right and the variation of applicable scenarios can be many. They are more about the *what* and the *how* than the why. The fundamentals are about the *why*. You can also develop new principles along the way. These aspects of principles make them generally not a good fit for the foundation that is you, so they are important but not fundamentals.

As previously mentioned, there was the event where my boss told me that the reason that I hadn't advanced beyond my imposed cap of a director level position was that I was too principled. That statement told me a lot about my boss and added more verification to things that

I already believed about the company and my situation. It, however, in no way made me give a second thought regarding changing my behavior or my principles. It is ironic that same person scored me very low on my review related to "integrity". I am not sure how a person that would make such a statement is in a position to judge others for their integrity. And, I would love to see their definition of integrity. I do not say these things because I am angry about a previous job, it is just such a good example of life that flies in the face of respect, trust, integrity, honor, and principles. I did not leave when I was told that; it actually was a learning opportunity as well as a validation of my principles.

The purpose of this section is not to tell you what your principles should be but rather to discuss the importance and use of principles. As you go through a list of principles, and even more so when you look at their implementation, you will inevitably find a need to prioritize the principles. This is okay. Priorities are perfectly okay, in fact, they are expected within a set of principles. Also, some principles may be isolated to particular use cases. As you blend priorities with principles, you may find that priorities define different sets of principles as well as help define the ranking within a set.

Remember that a principle is a rule or code of conduct that is focused on defining right from wrong. Principles can apply to work, to home, to your beliefs, or to anything that you choose and they can be quite granular. Principles are not likely to be based wholly on facts. They need to align with your fundamentals but unlike fundamentals are focused on the approach, the rules, and what is right rather than the why. Principles state what is right and maybe the rules for how to implement that, not why it is right. Of course, in building your principles, there is a basis for the principles that is collected and formed from your knowledge base.

It might help to give a very small sampling of some of my principles:

Planning before acting is essential. I use this one at work, at home, and everywhere. There are plenty of quotes and clichés that state this in various ways, but my principle is confirmed by experience. The results are far better when the time is taken to plan and consider the desired outcome even though I can't control all aspects of the outcome. It is a more efficient and effective use of my time.

I will not lie to protect myself or to make money. This is a specific rule for myself that I have not always followed in my life. Sometimes rules are made because of mistakes. I added parameters to lying because I still believe that I could and would lie to protect someone else.

There is something to be learned from every situation and from every person. I have a desire to be *better*. We will never know everything and one person cannot know all that is known. Others hold keys. Situations hold evidence of patterns. Self-assessment and introspection for the purpose of learning promotes growth not despair.

Write it down. The mind is not a steel trap that never loses anything and can recall anything at anytime. Some thoughts are fleeting. Writing it down is not just for the purpose of remembering but for forcing clarity of thought. Writing uses a different set of processes, which allows you to review and vet your thoughts in a different way. If you recall, the first step in creating fundamentals is to write down ideas so that they can be processed.

It is the responsibility of a manager to enable their employees. This is obviously a work-related principle but might have something deeper in generally how to treat people. People are more productive when they are respected, appreciated, and told why rather than do. In addition to being beneficial to the employee, it is clearly beneficial to the company.

Share your gifts and talents without looking for reward. Rewards can still come your way but it is not the purpose. In addition to the benefit to others and the world as a whole, the feeling of giving is wonderful.

Measure twice, cut once. I share this one for an idea of how granular and specific principles can be. I do a fair amount of woodworking and making a mistake in cutting too short can be a waste of time and money and moving fast when measuring has proven on occasion to be counterproductive.

Take the time to appreciate and enjoy what you have. Regardless of how much or how little you may feel that you have, looking at what you have rather than what you don't is a healing and calming experience. There are so many offshoots of this principle. What is it that I am chasing and for what purpose? If I have what I need, what am I doing with it? This does not apply to just "stuff"; it very much applies to people, emotions, health, senses, life, or anything.

I spent a fair amount of space on sharing a few of my principles and I offered a few indicators of why they came to be my principles. Despite one of my principles being write it down, I have not written down all of my principles. There are two primary reasons for that. Write it down does not mean that I write everything down; it means that it is beneficial. I write every day and I have had other priorities and with principles there will be priorities. The other reason is that I probably have well over a thousand principles by the time you get to all aspects of my life. I am hopeful that the diverse examples I gave you provided a bit more insight into how principles provide *your* personal rules of *right*.

Your principles can enhance the fundamental benefits of confidence and self-assurance, decrease the complexity of your decisions, and contribute to your inner peace.

The process of creating principles is similar to the process of creating your fundamentals with a few key exceptions. We talked about being consistent in the context of honor; it is also a good validation for principles. Samplings from Merriam-Webster's Dictionary:

> **consistent:** *"... free from variation or contradiction ... showing steady conformity to character ..."* [23]

Your principles should be able to withstand any scenario or they need to be refined. This may take some a long time; potentially a lifetime. Others may find that their principles are verified in a scenario and become stronger in conviction. This likely depends on how detailed your principles are.

I would suggest starting with the most basic core beliefs of what is right. The ones you currently believe are infallible and assess how you actually implement them. Unlike fundamentals, as your principles grow, there will likely be situations that will cause your principles to be in conflict and prioritization of principles will be required. In this sense, the honing process for principles is different than fundamentals. With fundamentals you would continue to "tune" the definition and scope of the fundamental to eliminate conflict. With principles, finding a conflict or an exception to the principle likely means that you have either identified a limited context or an entirely new principle.

Don't expect people to reward you for your principles or even recognize that you have them; they are for you. On the light side they provide you with guidance for your behaviors and steps to take; on the heavy side, they are your moral compass.

Chapter 2-9
INTEGRITY

Integrity is one of the initial fundamental ideas that spurred *honor* as a fundamental. The short and easy message in this is that integrity is essential to you having stability and others understanding who you are and what you stand for. Your integrity comes from consistent implementation of your principles and being a person of your word.

The first definition in Merriam-Webster's Dictionary is:

integrity: *"1: firm adherence to a code of especially moral or artistic values : INCORRUPTIBILITY..."* [24]

Merriam-Webster defines moral as:

moral: *"1 a: of or relating to principles of right and wrong in behavior: ETHICAL ... d: sanctioned by or operative on one's conscience or ethical judgment..."* [25]

Going a little further to Merriam-Webster's definition of right:

right: *"...being in accordance with what is just, good, or proper..."* [26]

That fits very well with where we are with principles and ties other concepts together nicely which is a piece of validation. I like the implications of incorruptibility as well.

Are you honest? Are you honest with yourself? What does it or would it take for you to lie or to commit a crime? So where does this leave us? People can always rationalize things that they do or think. People can and will make themselves believe that they are consistent and have a great deal of integrity. Applying the principles consistently is probably the only part of the definition that can be completely agreed upon. The subject of honesty implies that you tell the truth. The truth is based on what you believe to be the truth and that brings us to the discussion of fact and perception, which is a whole different topic. Again, it is clear that the fundamentals and their operational implementations are intertwined. This is a reason that the word consistent is probably a better fit than truth, but people can consistently lie and that is certainly not the intent of integrity.

If we go down the path of "just and good" for a moment, let's see where that leads. Most would likely agree that killing innocent people for fun would not fall in the category of good. What if killing 10 innocent people would be guaranteed to save 100 more innocent people? Is it just? Is it good? What if I change that to "might" save 100 people? This is obviously a situation that most would never face but we are all likely to be impacted by someone that would. The choice that is made in these situations is a personal choice and is not a universal absolute truth that mandates the *right* answer. Many will have an opinion and many will believe that they would have made a better decision, but until you are there in those circumstances, you may not know. Taking the premise that it is a personal decision of being *just*, then integrity is being compliant with a decision that you have defined. We are right back to being true to you which is what integrity and honor are really about.

We can only hope and pray that a very high level of integrity and quality facts leads the ones that make those decisions.

As another example, consider the process of creating and approving medications. It is very obvious that one of the side effects of almost any drug is death. Where does the rule come from that decides what percentage of deaths is okay in order to help some or most? This is why it is so important for you to be involved and understand as much as you can and make decisions for yourself rather than believing that some known or unknown person has your best interest in mind.

I have never faced a situation like the one described of choosing between tens or hundreds of people to live or die but I have faced very difficult decisions. I faced a situation of a runaway car with a small child alone in a car seat. The car ran into an electrical pole and a wire fell bouncing and snapping all around the car. Are you wrong if you don't try to rescue the child? Are you stupid if you try? Many will likely never face this situation either, but it was real for me. These are obviously extremes but addressing extremes helps you find your consistency, priorities, and your own operational definition of right and wrong.

There are hot topics that are clearly about right and wrong for most and there are clear differences in the definition. Abortion is a very good example. Some may avoid the subject, but for most, it is hard not to have an opinion and a belief in what is right and wrong. Do you know why you have the opinion that you do? On which of your principles and foundational elements is it based? If you apply those principles to other situations, are they consistently implemented? Is your integrity in tact? Did you hit a situation where multiple principles needed prioritization? Is the prioritization clear? This is asking a lot of questions, but these are the questions to ask yourself in order to help yourself.

All of these questions are self-assessment and discovery questions. They are not questions that someone else can answer for you, but someone from the outside can certainly aid you by pointing out what they may see to be inconsistencies. This should not be taken as judgment, even if it is intended that way, but rather something that you can use for yourself to personally understand your consistency and help you tune your fundamentals, apply your principles, and find your priorities.

Did this seem to drift off this chapter's topic of integrity? Your fundamentals and your principles are you, so of course continually addressing them is part of the topic. You cannot be true to something that is not well defined and up-to-date.

Are you having trouble seeing the difference between honor and integrity? I personally see integrity being subset of honor, but it is honestly not worth a debate over the difference. Since both are based on consistency and principles it is possible that, depending on your principles, they are the same. Some dictionaries use them as synonyms for each other. Both integrity and honor require a commitment to your principles.

Chapter 2-10
TRUST

Some equate trust with respect or set an *expectation* that trust will be both given and received. I do not believe either of these. You can respect someone and yet not trust all of his or her statements. Allowing for the benefit of the doubt (and if there is doubt, there is not complete trust), I cannot feel confident that the other person's perceptions, motivations, perspective on the context and relativity, and conclusions are the same that I would have. There is no assurance that they have all of the information that they need to make the appropriate conclusions for the perspective that they are offering. In this case, you could argue that you trust their intent but question their conclusion.

This absolutely does not mean that if you do not trust someone that you believe they are a liar or that they have some deceitful or malicious intent; far from that. Those things are not tied and tying them leads to problems on both sides of the equation. Making sure that you understand the information and taking responsibility for yourself is an obligation that you owe yourself. If you feel forced to trust everything that comes from someone, you will eventually find yourself in an unresolvable conflict because the information from two people that you trust will be in conflict. This will likely cause even more issues and create significant misunderstandings unless you can keep these concepts separate.

How does a doctor feel when you get a second opinion regarding their diagnosis or treatment plan? I can tell you from firsthand knowledge that their reactions vary widely from full support to indignation. Please do not let the reaction, or the concern over the reaction, of others keep you from validating your own decisions. It can be your decision to trust someone but it is *your* decision. This is not in conflict with the concept of love and putting others before you; it is adjacent to it. To put this in an exaggerated example, would you put your life ahead of your doctor's feelings? I hope not. When the matter at hand is your health, the context should be your health. When the counter to your health is the feelings of a person that you pay for services related to your health, the priorities should be fairly obvious. However, that type of consideration is often not contemplated and a gut reaction takes place that might not be in your best interest or even in alignment with your priorities and beliefs.

I recently had an encounter with a professional that did not end well. I engaged with a paid professional for an activity. There was something that happened during the engagement that raised question to the available information that he was using to make his recommendation. I asked if that information should be cleared up before proceeding and his recommendation was not to do that. At this point, I wish that I would have tried to clear it up myself, but I chose to trust this professional. As it turned out, going with his plan cost more and, with the information collected while executing his plan, turned out to be unnecessary. I do believe that this person honestly made the recommendation that he felt was best based on the information available. I also believe that I should have dug into it before proceeding.

When the work was complete and the information was available, I contacted the professional and stated that I was disappointed. I told him that I believe that he was not trying to misrepresent anything and that he made the recommendation he felt was best. I took responsibility for trusting and not following up myself on the information but that I was still disappointed. I pointed out the extra money that it cost me but did not ask for it back. By his reaction, you would think that my statements were the worst things that had ever been said to him. In fact, he pretty much said that. He stated that in all of his time in business, he had never been accused of anything negative in his work or had his integrity questioned. He believed that I accused him of cheating me out of the extra money that I spent. Even though I pointed out my accountability, clearly stated that I believe he made the recommendation he felt was best, and did not ask for any refund, he concluded that I was attacking his integrity and ended the relationship stating to never contact him again.

This is what happens when you tie so many concepts together and do not listen to the context of the other person. All I can do in that regard is to assess my actions and what I could have done differently. I could have done my research and I could have maybe made my statements in a different way, although they were factual. You can try but sometimes people will react the way they react and it is one of the reasons that other people's perceptions and reactions are not your sole motivator for your own decisions. Keep in mind that this person that had this reaction had the same mindset while making recommendations to me and he is a well-paid, well-educated individual.

It is worth taking this opportunity to point out the learning opportunity in this situation. How do we learn in this case and what do we learn? What I learn from this may be different than what you would learn. The potential conclusions are numerous. I could conclude that this is just a bad person that I should avoid, that I need to take more accountability, that this is just the way the world works, or I could discover more about how others' context and motivation impacts their decisions. All of these are not mutually exclusive and there are far more learnings that can come from this fairly small example, but it is an example of the opportunities that life brings to tuning your fundamentals and principles.

We have covered a lot of territory thus far without the typical definition lookup. We have touched on expectations, respect, feelings, acceptance, and many other topics that should not be tied directly to trust. Merriam-Webster's definition is as follows:

trust: *"1 a: assured reliance on the character, ability, strength, or truth of someone or something..."* [27]

As typical, this is the first of various definitions. There is even one that references hope as a synonym which I do not align with for this purpose, but there is a relationship. This definition does recognize that trust can be applied to someone or something. The something could be a person's words or actions, for example, and it is an *or* not an *and*.

All of these comments thus far might make you believe that I do not think that you should trust anyone. That is not the case. I do not believe in unearned trust or trust regardless of circumstances or topic. If you choose to trust your doctor, that is your call. Will you automatically trust your doctor's advice for finances should they offer it? Maybe you would but again, those decisions are yours to make and having lines around trust is not a bad thing. There are many times when trusting someone is not only warranted but necessary. If you have learned the integrity of a person through experience, you can trust that they will always do what they believe to be the right thing. If your priorities align with theirs and you know that they have more information than you do regarding the current matter, it is clear that trusting them is the logical and prudent thing to do.

As I previously stated, one of the lessons that I have learned is that credentials and labels should not create automatic trust and there are many reasons for that. Professionals make mistakes, can be misinformed, and generally do not know everything. They may even have their own agenda that does not align with yours. If they offer indignation in questions related to their knowledge, it is probably even more of an indication to move on. Nobody can know everything.

The bottom line is that trust is not only a choice; it is a precious commodity that should be treated respectfully and not handed out without careful consideration. Expecting trust is an arrogant position once you separate it from the other concepts. It is like saying to the person that you should make their decisions for them for whatever reason you think you should.

Integrity and honor are on the path to trust.

Well-tuned fundamentals and principles will allow you the peace of mind to trust yourself.

Chapter 2-11
RESPECT

It is a fairly common phrase to say, "show respect", but how do you show it and what is it? It might seem obvious to some, but with all words they take on a personal and societal perspective. Different Merriam-Webster dictionaries offered a varied and fair amount of defintions of respect. I chose examples from the Merriam-Webster Learner's Dictionary that in combination seem to provide a good basis for discussion:

> **respect:** *"1: to feel admiration for (someone or something) : to regard (someone or something) as being worthy of admiration because of good qualities ... 2: to act in a way which shows that you are aware of (someone's rights, wishes, etc.) ..."* [28]

Other definitions refer to authority figures and the law. Some other dictionaries provide a bit more indication of why and how respect is "earned", beyond stating *good qualities*. I will also note that I did not see one defintion that used the word *earned*.

These two sample defintions are taking different approaches. The first defintion focuses on how you *feel* about someone (admiration and regard). It also puts a condition on that feeling as being "worthy" of those feelings because of "good qualities". Since worthy, good, and qualities are all subjective terms, it would seem to leave it up to you and whether you feel like it.

The second definition acknowledges that there is action taken simply because of awareness of a person and mentions nothing of a judgment criteria for the respect. It is an action regardless of "worthiness". Respect, like other topics in this book, needs to be actionable, but should also incorporate some of the concepts from the first defintion. In the context of this book, respect likely combines love, honor, and some principles.

The action of giving respect can be done in many ways and, like love, it is not always acknowledged and does not require reciprocal action. Your actions that show respect and your criterion for respect are both personal decisions that can and should be driven by your fabric.

It is also true that, like many other actions, some people and some groups will put pressure on you with their perspective of what respect is, how to show it, and to whom. As with other external influencers, your fundamentals, knowledge base, and inner core will act as the processing filters. Let's take a further look at some of the considerations.

Earned Respect?

Many people will talk about *earning* someone's respect. I have said that myself. Earning respect can take a long time and situations can be different so the results in one situation vs. another may not be the same. How does someone earn your respect? It will likely depend on your fundamentals and your principles. Some principles may state that everyone deserves respect. Does that not undermine any value of respect? Maybe you believe that you don't have to earn it but you can lose it. Can you respect something that someone did but not respect the person, or vice versa? If you trust someone, is that respect? In order to respect someone must you trust them? So many questions!

Some people will default to putting some measurement criteria on respect; these include education, job, or job title. A doctor, a lawyer, a police officer, a teacher, a CEO, or a minister are all examples of jobs, titles, and education that some would say *earned* respect. How would you feel if you knew that person with the degree, that you respect, cheated their way through college? I think most would say that the title no longer deserves respect because they didn't *earn* it. With that, the measurement is not about the title but about the character. However, character is far more difficult to measure than a title.

So far, I have asked a lot of questions and not directly stated my opinion because I *respect* that you own your definitions and the answers to those questions. I am going to start sharing my opinion and some reasons why I have formed those opinions. My statement that I respect that you own your definitions and criteria is an indicator of one of my opinions. I probably don't know you, but I respect your responsibility for your decisions. I did not say that I did or did not respect you or your decisions. This means that each of the actions, abilities, responsibilities, and the people themselves are all separate objects of appreciation and potential respect for me. I can respect the actions of a person without respecting them.

The things that you can respect are about as diverse as the things you can love, if you remember that discussion. That conclusion for me also tells me that the respect of the actions is not the subject of this chapter. It is the respect of the person. Disconnecting them is very important to enable the ability to reconcile conflicts that will inevitably arise between a person and their actions.

For me, the people that I respect have *earned* my respect. Earning my respect cannot be done by others' criteria such as the titles or certificates that were awarded to them by someone else. I can respect that they took time to get that title, but the criteria for the title is not mine and there is so much that it does not tell me about the person. Respect has a very close relationship to honor. I do not have to agree with everything that a person says or thinks to respect them. For me, if they are thoughtful, consistent, and a person of their word, they will likely earn my respect over time. That does not mean that I treat people poorly before they have earned my respect. Remember I still respect their responsibility, the fact that they may have opinions, and any laws surrounding the interaction.

Respect with Age

Respect, or the lack thereof, has been an issue for a long time for the *elderly*. It seems worse today, but that may be because of my own age. Do you respect your elders (or the elderly) and, if so, why? Is it the pure time on earth or the willingness to observe and acquire knowledge over time that is the major factor between young and old? It is likely both. Just living on the earth with no observation and acquisition of knowledge is nothing other than getting old. Unfortunately, all that some see is someone that has lived a long time and has "old ideas". The ability to observe and collect knowledge without the time to do so is of little benefit as well.

What is even more challenging likely has little to do with knowledge or respect, it is about the ability to learn from someone without experiencing it yourself. That is a significant challenge, but it is one for which I still have hope or I would not be writing this book. I do not have false hope that there will be a major breakthrough and people will be able to completely learn without experience. The nature of the human race does not allow for that, but some have been able to learn from others without a personal experience and I can only hope for more.

The saying regarding history repeating itself is a good reason why it is important.

Age is a physical factor but is very difficult conceptually. Here are a few generalizations about age, the young, and the elderly. Youth have a hard time really comprehending that old people were actually young at one point. If they do think that they were young, they think of it as being so different that it is irrelevant. It is not. For many elderly people, it is hard for them to think of themselves as being old in the way they thought of "old" when they were young. When my mother was 85, she would get in the car and say, "I'm going to the home to help the old people." Even for myself, it is hard to comprehend that I am considered officially elderly. How many of you will now think of me differently because I have a label put on my age?

I believe that with age comes both respect and disrespect. There used to be a poster hanging in my room when I was in my late teens that said, "Don't trust anyone under 30", which was a parody of a 60's movement statement to the opposite. The picture on that poster was of an old man wearing gold chains and a peace sign around his neck. There were plenty of statments of age being a factor in songs in the young culture at that time, such as never wanting to get old. It was a bit ironic that a number of the leaders of that movement were bordering on 30.

Young people of every generation have likely stated, "Things are so different now than when you were young, you just don't understand." Things are changing and they always will, but there are fundamentals that never change. As with other statements that have been made related to learning, I respect that everyone has something to offer that I can learn from. Age brings more opportunity and more probability that there is something to share.

Respect does not Mean Blind Trust

Separating respect from trust is essential. Recognizing that there is a difference is the first step. Just because someone has your respect, whether earned or otherwise, does not mean that you do everything they say. It should mean that you listen and give due consideration, but when it comes down to it *even if* you are a young adult you own your decisions. Just because someone in *authority* or with a title told you to do something does not take you off the hook. This includes a number of roles that many do blindly trust. The most prevalent example is probably doctors. Doctors have had a lot of education and may have been practicing for a long time, but they are not you and they are human. There is no way that you can tell the doctor everything that is going on in your life and there is no way that you are the exact same as the masses on which their information and treatment is formulated. You owe it to yourself to challenge, to question, and to own the decision. It is you that will be impacted, not the doctor.

It may be that these previous statements sound like a recommendation not to listen to authority figures so there is a need to clarify that. Taking ownership for your own decisions is important, but there is also the reality of true authority and laws. If a policeman tells you to do something, you likely better do it even if you don't agree. This is referring to the legitimate scope of their role such as, "Put your hands on your head" or "Get out of the car", not something stupid like, "Go jump off that bridge". Parents of children should also be listened to and given the respect of the role. We are back now to the possibility that you don't respect the person, but you do respect their position on the current situation.

Giving respect to a *person*, not their title or actions, is a fabulous gift. Someone giving respect to you should be cherished.

Chapter 2-12
FRIENDSHIP

This is one of the relationships discussed in the fundamental of love. A case could be made for it being the most fundamental of all relationships, but before making that claim, let's go to the dictionary again. Since the definition of friendship starts with the state of being friends we will go to the definition of friend. This time we will look at Merriam-Webster's Student Dictionary:

friend: *"1:a person who has a strong liking for and trust in another 2: a person who is not an enemy <are you friend or foe> 3: a person who aids or favors something..."* [29]

Based on our current definition of trust, you don't have to trust a friend and you can trust people that are not friends. Since the first definition uses strong liking *and* trust, some would have a hard time accepting that. The second is even more questionable since it would seem that there are millions of people that are not your enemy that are also not your friend. The third seems to be a relationship between a person and *something*, which does not sound like friendship. It seems the definition of friend bombed so let's go back to friendship in Merriam-Webster's Dictionary:

friendship: *"...1: the state of being friends // they have a long-standing friendship   2: the quality or state of being friendly..."* [30]

In both cases we are pointed back to *friend*. Do any of the definitions work for your understanding and treatment of using the word friend or friendship? Remember that it is okay, if not an expectation of yourself, to not just accept what you are told. Is it wrong to use a dictionary as the source for definitions of words? Absolutely not; it is a great resource and more people should use dictionaries. Dictionary definitions are a good grounding point, but there are reasons that different dictionaries have different definitions. There is no absolute authority of the approriate definitions of words. You need to apply your context and consider how others communicate and what you are trying to convey to them. Learning and building knowledge flows through your fundamentals process. Treat a dictionary defintion as a positive external influencer.

There seems to be a general agreement across dictionaries that there is something more to friendship than just a person you know, but what that is varies across sources. Discussion of friendship shows up in the areas of sociology, psychology, anthropology, and of course philosophy, as well as many other areas.

Many other Internet searches resulted in adding a few common thoughts that it is mutual between 2 or more people and that it includes loyalty, faithfulness, honesty and pretty much every reference included trust.

Let's try one more source. *Nicomachean Ethics* by Aristotle, written around 350 BC, has Book VIII dedicated entirely to friendship. It is a very good read in my opinion. He talks about three types of friendship and one of those three that he refers to as *perfect friendship*.

Here is one excerpt from that book, "and it is among good men that trust and the feeling that 'he would never wrong me' and all the other things that are demanded in true friendship are found". [31]

True friendship is one of the three types of friendship that Aristotle defines. The other two types are friendship of utility and friendship of pleasure. He refers to the "true" friendship as friendship of the good.

As I said, Book VIII of Nicomachean Ethics is a very interesting read and I would encourage you to read it if you are interested.

From these various sources I am willing to accept that friendship includes trust. The impact of this is that, under this definition, people have far fewer friends than they might have stated without trust being included. Maybe this is the reason that I had an issue with it. I have people that I would have considered friends, but I have not determined whether or not I can trust them. These people are more than acquaintances to me but they have not reached a trust level. So I guess, for me, there is something between acquaintance and friend and there is no need to go deep into the definition of acquaintance.

Friends, as currently defined, is certainly not the type of "friends" that people have on social media. I'm not sure that many people's social media friends are even acquaintances. This leads to the conclusion that there are minimally these levels:

1. People with which you have some sort of connection but you know nothing about them
2. An acquaintance – implying that you are "acquainted" with them
3. A person that you might describe as a friend and have a relationship with of some form, but not to the level of a mutual trust and love (keep in mind the meaning of love from the fundamental section, this is not romantic love)
4. Friendship

I have taken you through a path of my own discovery and internal debate, so what is the conclusion and purpose of this chapter? Friendship is a relationship so, unlike the love fundamental, it cannot be one way. It is mutual love, trust and respect for each other. Wow! Yes, there are some people in my circle that meet that criteria but it is not hundreds of friends. Does that seem harsh to you? In order to have that mutual trust and respect, there needs to be personal experience that provides a strong enough indication in their dependability and an understanding of their principles to know that they will be there for you.

Friends are obviously another thing in your life to cherish and regardless of my comments in this chapter, I am sure you already knew that. If this chapter seemed like an exploration just to find a definition of friendship, I guess it was. Once you have the definition, the purpose, and the value, the function of a friendship is pretty obvious.

Part 2: Life's Realities

Chapter 2-13
SELF-PRESERVATION

Here is another topic that some might rank so high as to call it the purpose of life. I would not make that claim, but I do see it as a natural human response. The important aspect of self-preservation is when and to what degree it executes. What are your triggers?

It may be that you think of self-preservation as a self-defense mechanism against a physical attack or taking action to assure that your physical needs are met. You need to preserve your existence so you will make sure that you have food and are protected from harm. Those are clear self-preservation and self-defense instincts that are one of the realities of life. They are very likely, by instinct, very high on your priority list whether you have intentionally put them there or not.

These preservation instincts can sometimes be part of the inner core influences when it comes to decisions and they are usually subconscious influencers. They will impact decisions that involve any type of personal threat. As stated, much of that is instinct. Because they are instinctual, they can be difficult to manage. I say *manage* because it is not something that you necessarily want to suppress. Those instincts can literally save your life.

When *you* are in danger, instinctual fight or flight response may work well, but there are many situations that are going to include others. Others may be the source of the potential harm, the one being harmed, or the impacted people that are not directly part of the situation. All of those situations have an opportunity for management but they can still be very rapid fire and the need for instincts will prevail. Understanding yourself and building your patterns, that over time become subconscious decisions, can aid in those situations.

Because these types of self-preservation instincts are either part of you from the start or become that way over time, I want to focus on the self-preservation situations that are not physically harmful or block your existence.

I believe that there are self-preservation reactions that are called upon at what *might* be inappropriate times. The time to address that is at the trigger, not the reaction. I am sure you have heard the term "Don't be so defensive." Depending on your age, someone has probably said it to you. Being defensive is in some way a self-defense mechanism. Whether it was appropriately triggered is another discussion. Everybody has a *right* to defend him or herself, correct? Sure, if you are attacked, you can and should defend yourself but there are two conditions in that statement that are often *exaggerated*. Are you defending your "good name", your beliefs, your opinions, or do you even know what you are defending?

If you are attacked is key. The perception of being attacked is a growing question because we seem to be in an increasing spike of so many people *feeling* as though they are being attacked. Since one's perception is a trigger, something that is not an actual attack at all can be perceived as an attack and trigger the self-defense mechanism. As those triggers become more and more sensitive and more and more people are triggered to self-protection, an escalation of a defensive nature is inevitable. Soon it is impossible to have a conversation because so many *feel* attacked and consequently *defend* themselves. Do you think someone is implying something bad about you? Did you not like a word that they used (having no idea why they used it)?

We have talked about the sensitivity of the triggers and how that can create issues; let's look at the defense. If the triggers can become exaggerated, so can the defensive actions. There is a saying that "the best defense is a good offense." Whether it is a proactive offense or the defense turns to an attack, there is risk of becoming the attacker rather than the defender.

When you combine the sensitive triggers with the excessive "defense", there is trouble brewing. From the outside, this combination no longer looks anything like self-preservation. If you feel that you are always in or need to be in a defensive position, it may be time to look at it from a different perspective. This not about paranoia, but that could be an elevated example. This is referring to always being on guard because others are negative, don't understand, say (or even think) mean things, or any number of non-life-threatening actions. Part of the purpose of this book is to know yourself and be yourself by the use of the fundamental circle which promotes self-esteem and inner peace. The defensive scenario that was just described sounds nothing like inner peace.

If you look inward rather than outward, which is sometimes very difficult to do, you will have a different perspective. Others do not define you and therefore have no basis for judging of you. They may show their ignorance of you and who you are, but that is their shortcoming and not yours. On the flip side you may not understand or know them. This is not a statement encouraging you to be an introvert. It is about finding balance, accountability, and recognizing what you can control.

The short story on the inappropriate or even offensive reactions is that they are not a well-calculated or effective use of your time and energy and it is fighting for *outcomes* over which you do not have control.

Chapter 2-14
SUCCESS

This is another topic that, either by design or by default, people may have as their purpose in life. The validity of that may depend on the goal. Most think of success as something that is defined and acknowledged by someone else, or very often by "society". What do *you* typically think, or think that most think of when someone says, 'That is a successful person"? Many people think of something to do with money or a title. A billionaire, a doctor, a lawyer, or a CEO might all be seen as being successful. It is not shameful that people think that; it is how the term has been used.

Money and title are not however the way that most people, when faced with the most important things in life, would see as the things that define their life. If you succeed at the things that are the most important to you in life, are you not successful?

The dilemma for most is going to be breaking the dependency on the perception and acknowledgement of others. People have been conditioned to look for that approval and recognition as well as it just plain feels good. There is another chapter on approval and acceptance so I don't want to spend too much time on that, but this is a place where they clearly overlap. Another overlap chapter of success is the purpose of life. These are a couple of heavy hitter chapters that impact success. What is left?

It's time to check the dictionary and see what Merriam-Webster says:

> **success:** *"1 a: degree or measure of succeeding   b: favorable or desired outcome, also : the attainment of wealth, favor, or eminence   2: one that succeeds..."* [32]

Well, there is wealth and another self-referencing definition, so we need to try succeed:

> **succeed:** *"...a: to turn out well   b: to attain a desired object or end // students who succeed in college..."* [33]

Is this what you expected? It is better than I expected. So much pressure is put on success when the definition is achieving an objective, especially when others define it. We talked about goals earlier in this book, and who sets our goals? We each set our own goals based on our fundamentals. In other words, we have the opportunity to define our own criteria for success. That is good but it comes with risks.

A couple of key guidelines are important when setting your goals and objectives. Consider the things that are important to you (not others) and remember what you can control. Setting an objective for an *outcome* rather than an action is an objective that is significantly out of your control. You can hope for those things but hope is not a very safe goal. Stretch goals are fine, but stretch yourself, not factors for which you have no control. There is no reason for you to fail because of circumstances outside of your control. You are in control of your actions (decisions) not their results (outcomes).

Some examples are in order. Say that I have a desire that thousands of people will benefit from this book. I don't even have a way to measure that and I sure can't control it. I could change it to I want 10,000 people to read it. I can't control that either, but I could have an impact. The first thing that I need to do is write the book and that is in my control. That is a good goal. I can break that down further into smaller increments and say that in order to achieve this goal, I am committing to write a minimum of 5 days a week. I can measure that and it is a choice that I make. I can say that I have success every week or not and can say that I wrote the book when it is done and that would be successful. I can also set a goal to build a marketing and distribution plan. The book might not be "successful" but I would be. Will others call me successful? I would guess most would not use that label unless social or financial popularity is achieved, but that is for them. I care about my personal success and people that care about me care about that success and what else really matters?

Since most people will probably not write books, here is another example. Remember that your goals should align with your fundamentals and principles so I would not pick being wealthy, but for the purpose of this example I am going to start with that. Success would be defined by being wealthy but you do not have full control of that. You might be getting the gist of this, that a good goal for defining success is the how and not the what. You can start with the *what* but your goal and measurements are the *how*.

Let's say you start with, "I want to be rich!" First you would define rich, then assuming it's a measurable amount of money, you would create the steps that you could control to increase the possibility of that happening. If, along with that, it included a particular job that could help attain that, you would create the plan for the job. Would it be school? Would it be an apprenticeship? Would it be networking, online training, or is it investments, regardless of the job? Maybe your first step is to research the various ways that people become wealthy. There are so many things that you can do that will *increase the possibility*. You can be wrong about the outcome or even the best way to go about it and still be successful. That is going to seem wrong to some, but hinging your success on hope, luck, or other things out of your control, seems wrong to me.

This does not mean to just set easy achievable goals and call it a success. Align with your fundamentals and your principles and be true to yourself. Just *do not* hold yourself accountable for others' perceptions. *Do* hold yourself responsible for selecting and achieving your goals, and claim your success as well as build your self-esteem and self-respect.

Chapter 2-15
CONTROL

There are some that wish to control everything and those that wish to control nothing. Neither is completely possible. You control your actions or lack of actions; what you cannot control is the outcome from those actions. It is the nature of many of us to want to control our life; many of us understandably try. As we have discussed, we cannot control the outcome of our actions, we can only increase the possibility that the outcome will be our desired outcome. That is not a bad thing. It is the life we live.

The Serenity Prayer comes to mind here. While it uses the word "'change" rather than "control", the sentiment and the challenge is the same. It is important that we understand what we can and should control and what we cannot. The issues and challenges with control are even deeper than these comments. The concept of control intersects with almost all aspects of life. In addition to your desirable self-control, there is your attempt to control others and others' attempt to control you. The word *attempt* is used for a reason.

Control Freak

Healthy control has a reasonable scope of trying to control your own life, environment, and well-being. Some things cannot be controlled or foreseen, but taking the initiative to make things happen *for you* is an underlying component of the feeling of accomplishment, success, accountability, and self-respect. That is all healthy.

The power freak will attempt to control others. Some degree of that, a very small degree, might be expected in certain positions such as someone whose role it is to legally maintain order. That is just a role and not a power freak. This seems to have turned from talking about control to talking about power. In this context they are likely the same. There are plenty of terms, clichés and quotes that go along with this concept such as the term *power hungry.* Sir John Dalberg-Acton is credited with saying *"Power tends to corrupt, and absolute power corrupts absolutely."* [34]

Much of that power is viewed as the ability to control. In fact, one of Merriam-Webster's definitions of power is as follows:

power: *"... possession of control, authority, or influence over others..."* [35]

The joining of control and power is a vicious circle that grows rapidly. The thirst for power utilizes corrupt methods of control. The resulting ability to control justifies the corruption and feeds the power. And with more power comes more ability to control, and so it grows.

Just Tell Me What to Do

There are those of us that would say, "Just tell me what to do." These people are either tired or lazy. Maybe that's a little harsh? I know that sometimes, depending on the decision to be made, there is just not the energy or emotional bandwidth to make a decision and that can occasionally happen, but should not be a way of life. In case it is not obvious why there is reference to making decisions in a chapter about control, it is because making decisions *is* your control.

Making decisions and putting some thought into it is a responsibility and obligation. That might feel like too much pressure for some. While it is an obligation, more importantly it is one of the most significant freedoms that we have. It is one of those inalienable rights; regardless of who you are and where you are, you have the freedom of choice. That is your control of you.

Manipulation and Morality

Manipulation other than the physical type is some form of control. It is an attempt to mislead, misrepresent, or manage someone else through manipulation. The method of control gets back to a number of other topics including fact vs. perception, learning, trust, knowledge, and wisdom. The antidote to being manipulated is knowledge or at least the desire for it. We have discussed the sense of *right* and morality being driven by principles, but there are external influencers that can inhibit that. In this case, that external influencer is attempting to control your decisions.

People exert their control in various ways. Some are long-term strategies and some are just short-term deceptions. The long-term strategies are the hardest to detect. Politicians and politics in general are good examples of longer-term strategies. The term "spin" is nothing more than manipulation. Someone wants to put a spin on something so you see that thing in a way that is better for them. Politicians, the government, and corporations do it all the time. That is not a conspiracy thought it is an accepted practice. One could question its morality but it is real. The idea that it is an accepted practice is all the more reason to be aware of it and take responsibility for what you accept. If someone can control what you think, what you believe, or your opinions, they have gained power and that power is not likely for your benefit. It is control via manipulation.

Other External Control Methods

Some will attempt control with intimidation or use control created out of existing power such as those in a role that can make laws or rules whose purpose is to control your behavior or actions. Think city council, the board of a homeowner's association, or the management in companies. The world is full of rules for the purpose of controlling you. Of course some controls are required for a civilized society such as the law against murder, but laws and rules go far beyond that. Be respectful, but be aware.

The evolution of manipulation for the purpose of control is lies. If someone needs to control someone else, the line between manipulation and lies is very thin. The purpose of the control is power and power is a very strong force against any moral or ethical opponent.

Summary

Infringement on someone else's ability to have their own thoughts might be one of those things that are blocking your sense of self and ability to understand yourself. On the other hand you are responsible for yourself, so if someone lies to you or manipulates you, they may have been wrong, but you have some accountability. Does that accountability put a different perspective on trust? Have you considered that you are responsible for the ones that you trust?

There is an important relationship between control and responsibility. These terms can seem like opposing concepts but they are not. How can you take responsibility if you don't take control? The key is what you attempt to control. You cannot control *all* aspects of an *outcome* and therefore are not responsible. You *are* responsible for your actions and control of yourself.

Your control of self is essential to your decisions. Be aware that others will attempt to control outside of themselves. Any attempt to control outside of yourself should be assessed against your fundamentals and principles. Sharing your knowledge, learnings, and opinions, is not the same as an attempt to control. Keep learning, as knowledge is your best defense against the external forces of control.

Chapter 2-16
EXPECTATIONS

Why do we have expectations? Why do we need them? We like to know the future, but clearly any prediction of the future is not a fact. An expectation gives us the ability to plan without guarantee but with some level of probability. In that sense it is related to trust.

Who sets the expectations? It is great when someone else sets the *appropriate* expectations but often that is not the case. The result may often be false expectations. False expectations can be one of the negatives in life. Even when someone else sets expectations, unless there is trust, the result is still likely that you set your own expectations. Someone may tell you something that is going to happen but it is your choice to decide whether or not that sets your expectations. It does have a great deal to do with trust but, to broaden it further, it is really about you taking the accountability for your expectations. You allow the expectations to be set.

As an example, the car dealership tells you that your car will be ready by 4:00 PM today. You may choose to believe that and make plans around that because they are a dealer and you have no reason to believe that they could be wrong. If you look deeper and recognize that you have been using them for service for the last 15 years and they have always delivered, you have even more reason to choose to believe them because you have some history that has built some level of trust. If you have never been to them before, you might think that the delivery time is just 4 hours away and they do this for a living, and they have a reputation to protect. On the other hand, you may have used them before and they have always been off on their estimates or you may have heard from others that their reputation of timely and quality work is in question, but they are the only game in town. The point of this is the recognition of your own accountability for expectations. How much are you willing to put on that other person's word?

So far, we have talked about expectations initiated by others, but there are other expectations that are both important and very prevalent; they are the ones that we initiate and set for ourselves. It is pretty common to expect an outcome for an action that you take. We have talked about this in many ways, but the bottom line is that we do not have full control of the outcome. If I say hi to someone, they will say hi back. If we are pleasant to someone, they will be pleasant back. If I twist hard on the cap of a jar, it will open. If I work harder than another person, I will be rewarded for that. Daily, there are probably hundreds of opportunities for us to consciously or subconsciously set our own expectations, likely with every decision we make. Every expectation is another opportunity to be let down or feel like you have failed. We can increase the probability of our expectations being fulfilled, but too many factors impact things that we cannot control.

There is another aspect of expectations. That is in the sense that somebody owes you something for whatever reason you think. You *deserve* it. Unless there is a contract with someone, I'm not sure that anybody *deserves* anything. In this case, if people used the term as defined by Merriam-Webster, I would use the word more and not have the opinion that I do:

deserve: *"...to be worthy of..."* [36]

That is not, however, the way that I hear it being used. If you do a general Internet search for definitions of deserve, you will find results that mean that someone has a right to or deserves something. I believe these are the definitions of the word that many mean when they say deserve. These are the definitions that I generally do not buy.

People work, they take positions, they make choices, there are consequences, and sometimes (maybe many times) life is not fair. Saying that someone deserves something can have a flip side that someone else does not. That is not the case for your ability to make decisions, but since that is something that nobody can take from you, there is no reason to state that you deserve it. You *deserve* to make decisions and you can.

While there is allowance for deserving things under contract such as repayment of a loan, applying the laws, or constitution of a country, that is not the most typical use of deserve. The prevalent usage is that because I am who I am, I did what I did, or my parents did what they did, somebody owes me something, "I expect it." I deserve to control the outcome of my life, I deserve to go to college, I deserve a nice car, I deserve to be happy, I deserve to have whatever you have, on and on and on. I believe that people do things that make them worthy of a result, whether that is a good or bad result. I do not believe that they should *expect* it. While expecting it can lead to disappointment, it also can enable a viewpoint of entitlement. Entitlement can lead to being passive in life and expecting and waiting for something to happen that you deserve. Do something to increase the probability and if that doesn't work, as long as you still have hope, do something else.

Using the knowledge acquired over time to set your expectations is a wise move. It does not guarantee accuracy but your chances are better. Expectations may be best viewed as desire, hope, or degrees of perception probabilities. It is also very appropriate to call people out on not meeting expectations that they have set. The concepts of integrity, responsibility, accountability, trust, and respect still exist.

Chapter 2-17
EQUALITY

I have *tried* to stay out of social issues in order to not date these writings as I believe the concepts within this book are, for the most part, timeless. In this case however, I cannot resist the reference to social issues happening today as I suspect that they will persist or, at a minimum, be cyclical. When many people talk about equality they refer to equal results regardless of other factors. I find this concept ludicrous. Life is complex and to put it bluntly, shit happens. There are reasons that different people get different outcomes and some of them are within their control and some of them are not. Let me clarify that this is not talking about prejudice; it is about the lack of prejudice. Lack of prejudice is as close as I can get to a reasonable definition of equality.

When talking about equality, the word fairness comes to mind. A solution is seen as legislating fairness which leads to someone defining *fair* in a law. You could say that being fair is a moral issue. We have discussed the concept of morality and how it is a personal definition and mandating morality is not something that can work.

Another more holistic view of fairness is simply that *life is not fair*. So what! This is not a statement against equal opportunity or "fair" treatment of people, but life from its beginning is not fair. We do not have a choice in which country we were born, or to what family status or any of those things that so many strive for. It is not fair! No it is not. It is what we have. How would you go about making those things fair from the beginning? I understand the implication that fair is synonymous with equal and that is the point. Neither equal nor fair can mean that everything or everyone is the same because they are not. It is a fact that people are born in different countries and into different family statuses. Because of those differences, you can argue that life will be *easier* for some but now you are into a question of the definition and context of "easy". Is easy the objective of equality?

I have been in many debates regarding equality and it always comes down to the definition and expectation of implementation. If you look at dictionary definitions you will see words such as same and identical. From this standpoint, we are clearly not equal. That is not what is meant by many, so in conversation we cannot use the discussion of equality without defining its meaning and even more importantly, its scope.

Take another view of this and say that fairness is actually about not being superficial in decisions, but rather getting to the substance before making a decision. That seems like a logical statement. "Don't judge a book by its cover." [37] Correct? Let's play this out in a literal analogy.

There is a library that has a project to stock the best 100 books of the year. They start their discovery process for finding the books through a polling and judging process and end up identifying 500 books. To reduce the number of books, they eliminate all books that have bicycles or cars on their cover. Logical people wonder what is going on and understand that is not fair and has nothing to do with the best books. A protest is formed and demands are made to include books with cars and bicycles on their cover. In fact, the demand is made that 80% of the books selected must include bicycles or cars on their cover. What? I thought the argument was that using the image on the cover was not a legitimate criterion for judging the best book. What happens to the great books that now cannot be read and the people that cannot read them?

Somewhere the purpose and the whole argument went out the window and those that demanded to not use the cover are now insisting on using the cover. It would seem logical that the solution should be that the judges are not allowed to use the cover. They may not even be allowed to see the cover because the point is to stop talking about and thinking about the cover and judge by content.

People will be judged, measured, and impacted by their actions and abilities and rightly so. Equal treatment for the same actions and abilities and equal opportunity to attempt is what should be desired. An equal result regardless of effort is just plain crazy. Believing that all people have equal abilities is just as crazy. Some people are stronger, or taller, or smarter, or faster and any number of abilities that are inherent in who they are. How you use and improve your abilities should be up to you.

What should not be expected or draped in a false veil of equality is that all people get equal results. All people make the same amount of money regardless of how hard they work, all jobs that *require certain abilities* are filled, not based on ability but rather on the things that actually define prejudice. The percentage of the police force and of doctors MUST equal the population of males and females, and of ethnicities, and of religious beliefs. Forcing those factors *creates* prejudice rather than addresses it and it is a disservice to all involved. How will you feel if your doctor is inferior to what they should be because the person with the most ability was not allowed to practice? How many lives will be at risk if we fail to recognize and reward the abilities?

I believe that the civil rights movement of the 60's had a solid message about the concept of equal opportunity. Martin Luther King Jr.'s famous "I have a dream" speech on the steps of the Lincoln Memorial referred to not being judged by color but rather by character. This speech is worth a listen or a read.

That is easy to get behind that sentiment and I support it wholly! The speech did not indicate that they would not be judged, but rather that they would be judged on the important aspects of who they are. Prejudice makes no logical sense and shows a shallowness of thought. However, that word has morphed into what one could argue to be greed, but I don't think that completely explains it. There are political movers and shakers that are promoting their agenda and drawing support by promising free stuff rather than opportunity. Free stuff has an appeal on the surface, but for those that are willing to look even one layer down, it is a charade. Somebody pays. Somebody works. I know that this has gone way off the rails here but this is not only relevant to the topic of equality, it is a reality of life today. Can you see how ships pass in the night due to misuse or misunderstanding of words, manipulation of perceptions, opinions, greed, self-preservation, and pretty much all of the life topics that are in this part of the book?

I want to be clear that the equality and prejudice that I am talking about is not just racial. It is *anything* that is superficial. It includes anything that is not the *ability* or *character* relevant to the situation. This could be weight, height, age, ethnicity, sex, hairstyle, eye color, your name, size of your nose, and anything that you can possibly imagine. I understand that all of these superficial characteristics are not on the same level and some may be within your control and some not, but all are superficial. A predetermined decision based on *any* superficial characteristic is prejudice and is not equal opportunity.

Equality is one of those principles, which some choose to live by and some choose to abuse. Even when there is equality in opportunity, there are factors that can lead to unexpected and "unfair" results. Expect that life is not fair and the outcome of every effort is not always rewarded. Sometimes the results cannot be explained and sometimes there are circumstances controlled by others that manipulated the results. Stand strong against that manipulation. Be honest and be you!

Chapter 2-18
GREED

How much is enough? Where greed applies, nothing is enough. I suspect that *everything* is not even enough. Taking it to the extreme, in order to have everything, everyone else would have nothing and with nothing, everyone else would die. Okay, that wasn't too realistic, but the point is that greed cannot be about what you get if getting everything does not satisfy it. Greed is referenced in the topic of equality but greed is not caused by a search for equality or fairness; it is quite contrary to that.

If greed can never be satisfied, what drives it? I suspect that greed is similar to power in that *more* is what matters. Greed wipes out the ability to appreciate what you have and what surrounds you. It is the acquisition of more that is important.

Time to go to Merriam-Webster's Dictionary again:

greed: " *a selfish and excessive desire for more of something (such as money) than is needed ...* " [38]

The defintion of greed leads to looking up selfish:

selfish: *"1: concerned excessively or exclusively with oneself : seeking or concentrating on one's own advantage, pleasure, or well-being without regard for others..."* [39]

This is starting to sound a bit Hedonistic. Unless you are of the Hedonism philosophy, it is not likely that you can see a positive aspect of greed; I cannot. If you look at the precise language of "more than is needed", one should raise the question of how much is actually needed. Besides most people not being practicing Hedonists, most people also want more than they *need*. Does that mean that most of us have unpleasant, non-admirable traits?

This discussion is not going in this direction to make people feel bad or guilty. By the explicit phrase in the definition of *more than is needed*, there is likely greed in all of us. Some of that is healthy motivation. The first part of the definition is key, in that it states *excessive*.

Part 2 of this book is about realities of life and implementing our fundamentals. As we look at greed in the context of other chapters of this book, it could come into the conversation of most of them. Many chapters have a lot of crossover with others, but this one is different. We have talked about *what, how,* and *why* from the beginning and the fundamentals are the why and Part 2 is focused on mostly the what and how. Greed is a *why*. As we said, greed has no end and no success; it is a driver.

Desire and motivation getting out of hand become greed and it can take over and become the *why*. It is something to keep in check with your fundamentals and principles.

Part 2: Life's Realities

Chapter 2-19
ACCOUNTABILITY & RESPONSIBILITY

Taking responsibility for your actions; what a unique and faded concept that seems to be. Accountability and integrity are certainly related. You holding yourself accountable is certainly an aspect of Honor. If you find yourself in a situation where something negative has happened, do you look to yourself to understand what you may have done to influence the situation? If you are one of the few that would do that, would you then speak up and tell others involved? That number is even smaller. Once again, the reason for looking at yourself is not to blame or shame yourself, it is to learn. Did you make the best decision that you could and still be you? If so, there may be learning opportunity but there is no reason for blame or feeling failure. This does not include the situation when unanticipated or unexpected things happen, but rather when there is a *direct* cause and effect relationship between action and result.

There is a growing mentality of "if you don't get caught, it didn't happen". This is not meant to imply that all people that do this are evil and are plotting this approach; rather that society and the culture is evolving to that thinking. The intention has been to keep this book focused on aspects of life that are not specific to a point in time and I find myself drifting to current social trends. I have two sides pulling at me and it is difficult to be true to both. I want the message to be timeless but I cannot ignore the power of real-life examples of today. Even if they become history, which I hope some do, learning from history is important.

This is where people can find conflict in good intentions. It was obvious to me in college when I was taking psychology and philosophy at the same time and found that many times they were conflicting. The conflict was not only in approach but also in conclusions. It was very hard to hold to one side or the other and I believed that to be a healthy approach. There were aspects of both that had value even when they were in conflict. My professors did not agree. Related to keeping current events out of this book, I will continue *trying* to minimize any current events and only use them as references rather than a basis for my statements. I will take the *responsibility* for my actions.

Various dictionaries use responsibility to define accountability and vice versa. This would imply that they are synonymous or very close. The only nuance, when digging into the root of the words, is that responsible references the cause and accountable references the acceptance of the cause. "I was responsible for causing that and I accept the accountability." The definitions never really state this difference, but it seems as though the responsibility is the action prior to an event and accountability is after. That's enough time on that. For this purpose we can assume them to be *too close to call*.

Let's take the affirmative or positive view on this topic. If you take responsibility for your actions and for the results of your actions, you can grow in many ways. The sense of honor can be a powerful feeling that provides an internal sense of satisfaction and worth. Even if the results were negative (in most cases, not intended to be negative), it provides value to yourself in being honest and honorable, knowing that you are not hiding something or holding something that may eat at you.

William Shakespeare's Hamlet quote, "to thine own self be true"[40] seems appropriate here. This is clearly not a new concept. Believing in yourself is extremely important to your growth and the value you can provide to others. You cannot believe in yourself if you are not truthful with yourself. If you believe in yourself, knowing that you will take accountability, it can over time alter your thought process and therefore your decisions, knowing that actions have consequences.

This is referring to self-imposed accountability, but it can be that others will hold you accountable as well. When you hold yourself accountable, there is no threat or feeling of being *caught* or *found out* and the inner peace that comes from that is wonderful. That type of approach and consistency is also the type of action that will build others' trust in you.

The accountability learning opportunity should not be missed. It is far too often that people do not associate cause and effect. Without understanding what influenced or caused a result, there is not only a missed learning opportunity but there is also a risk of building a mindset of "no consequences".

Suppose a business started losing money and nobody *looked* for the cause. There may be a tendency to blame things that could not possibly be the fault of the business such as the economy, or the other business that is "stealing" your clients, or the weather, or any number of other things. The business could have "missed" the fact that they reduced their marketing spend by 75% and they raised their prices by 30%. Who is going to take the responsibility to see that the correlation between cause and effect takes place? Accountability is good for the mind and the soul.

You might see what seems to be a conflict with the previous statements regarding not being able to control the outcome and looking for a direct cause and effect before blaming yourself. This is not a conflict; it is about finding an *honest* balance. The concepts of fact and perception certainly come into play as well. You may ultimately not know some definitive answers especially when multiple influencers are in play. However, there should be an honest and objective assessment of the cause related information. Remember the purpose is not blame but learning. We could probably put hundreds of examples out there to try to show ideas of how to land on a good answer, but we are not going to. It is ultimately up to you and your fundamentals to take the input and decide. Here are a few guidelines:

- Consider as much information as possible.
- Rank the information by the probability of being true.
- Be honest with yourself regarding your responsibility; only you know your intent.
- Avoid conjecture and playing the IF game of what you think could have happened IF something else had happened.
- Don't look further than one step away from the event. Daisy-chaining multiple cause and effects is too prone to error and is *very* unreliable.
- Expect that there may be multiple potential candidates of the cause with different probabilities; partial accountability is still accountability and still learning.

Chapter 2-20
APPROVAL & ACCEPTANCE

There are many people that live their life for approval and acceptance. In some cases it is to the extent of being their life's purpose. People can obviously pick anything that they want for their life's purpose, but the acceptance from others is such an uncontrollable target and cannot be achieved en masse. There will always be someone that doesn't like you. Sorry if that burst your bubble.

Social media and the easy access to so many people in such a near real-time experience has made this a bigger and more prevalent issue. This can be an issue, not because acceptance or approval from others is bad or evil, it is because it goes to an extreme for so many and inhibits people from being themselves. They end up serving at the whim of others and that whim is ever changing.

Approval and acceptance and its rating of popularity has been part of our nature for a long time. Popularity is rewarded in a number of ways. In addition to the emotional rush that can be gained by many people "liking" you, popularity gets monetized. People get money for being popular. Number of hits, likes, views, etc. all can add up to dollars. The music industry is, in a significant way, a popularity contest. Of course being popular is the result of a "hit" but there are so many great talents that are not popular. Many artists will pull out all the stops in order to manipulate the popularity rather than focusing on the music. That is not a judgment or even a negative comment, it is just a reality of the music industry.

People that are well liked and are accepted will go further in almost any career. Someone will not likely hire you if you don't make a good impression. There are so many classes and books on every aspect of being accepted, and being liked in all aspects of life. Even as a child, it is a very common feeling of children to want their parent's approval. I remember the sinking feeling if I felt that I disappointed my parents. Approval is built into our being from the beginning. If you have children, how many times have you said "Good job"?

People like to be recognized for who they are and what they do, and being told that someone likes you vs. they don't like you feels better. Recognition for good work is something that helps many people continue and provides them with validation. This is at least where it starts and that is an honest and healthy feeling. Recognition for hard work and recognition for the extra effort are results that reinforce your efforts. You did something for the reasons aligned with your fundamentals and principles and on top of it, as a bonus, you get recognition for it. It feels good.

It took a lot of explanation to cover some of the background of approval and why it feels good. It will take very little to cover why it can be very detrimental. It becomes problematic when the *purpose* (the *why*) of your action is approval. It can be hard to buy into but the most important and powerful approval is your own. This is an extremely difficult concept for many to accept and even harder to implement. If you can keep approval, acceptance, and popularity on the result side of your actions rather than the cause side, you will have preserved your ability for self-respect and inner peace.

Chapter 2-21
WORRY & FEAR

Worry, worry, worry. What can be written about worry? What if people don't like it? What if a word is misspelled? What if...? For most people, worrying is a *series* of what-ifs.

Consideration was given to combining worry with the chapter on fear but on the surface they seemed too different. They are different in that they can be triggered in different ways and the intensity and acuteness *might* generally be different. However, as I started writing, looking at definitions, researching further, and examining my own experiences, I found that I couldn't talk about one without talking about the other. When the information would be 80% redundant by separating them, it was time to combine them.

Some of the minor differences between them include the idea that worries can jump rapidly across what-if scenarios where fear is usually more stable on a specific object, thing or event. Fear is also an emotion or response that can be triggered by real danger; there is no what-if in that situation. There *is* something to be afraid of.

Many times worry and fear go together and worry can trigger fear. The definitions of both include the term *anxiety*. Both can inhibit, if not destroy, your ability to utilize your fundamentals and can completely disrupt the circle.

The major commonality of worry and many fears is the unknown. What is going to happen? Worry is based on concern of something that might happen and one of the most devastating fears is also based on anticipation. Some unknowns may be based on anticipation of something that was previously eminent. An example would be fear of snakes. A person that is afraid of snakes will certainly be afraid if they see one and they may have an acute reaction, but they will likely also *anticipate* the fear. Avoiding going places where there is more likely to be snakes can escalate to avoiding places where there *could be* snakes, to avoiding places that are highly improbable for snakes. Decisions about vacations, the purchase of a house, a job, an education, anything can be impacted by that ongoing anticipation. Some may call this irrational, but fear is *real*.

Fear is one of the most powerful emotions in life. It directly drives decisions and actions and has the power to create *alternate realities*. The famous quote from Franklin D. Roosevelt's inaugural address is, "the only thing we have to fear is fear itself." [41] This is an inspiring and supportive statement for a president and I agree with the general sentiment. The cycle of building the fear of fear is probably the most invasive and disabling type of fear. This does not mean there are not real things to fear, because there are. There are real dangers in the world. Most of them are not eminent, but the acknowledgement of their existence can keep you aware of things around you. Being aware of them is not the same as them being frequently or constantly in your face like the fear of fear can be. This more detailed explanation of fear does not make for a good presidential speech.

As I look at examples from my past, I can say for sure that the anticipation of fear is horrible. It can make you physically ill, change your perception of reality, change the way you live, and cause you to miss things that you would have loved to do. Those fears have a way of growing and attaching themselves to activities that might be related, as well as to other fears or negative events. This negative spiral can easily get out of control. If you imagine the worst experience that you have had and convince yourself that the experience or the emotion that is attached to it *might* be triggered by an upcoming action or event (especially ones that you know little about), you are quickly in a spin toward the inevitable belief that it *will* happen.

Fears can be diagnosed phobias (mostly self-diagnosed) or an anxiety disorder, but regardless of the label, it is *real*. Some may say there is nothing to be afraid of. Okay, that just solved the issue. I hope I don't need to say that was a facetious comment but it was. Because some of these behaviors can be mental health concerns, I am not suggesting that this chapter will solve your fears; it will not. I also would not suggest that you use this information to override any type of treatment. I offer this information about my experiences and the results and impacts that I have seen in hope that it can help others.

One of the biggest things that I learned through my journey was that I was not alone. Society today is increasing the likelihood for anxiety issues. There is pressure to be accepted, to be successful, to be normal, and the stress caused by the news of the day that can only seem to talk about the hatred and evil that is creeping everywhere.

I am not ashamed of my fears and that is one of the things that has helped me. My fears are not completely gone but I am in a *much* better place today, even though there are still some fears that alter my behavior. My behavior and decisions are no longer altered in such a way that compromises my fundamentals or principles. Fear is not a fundamental, nor is it a principle. If it were, it would undermine the whole purpose and effectiveness of the fundamentals. Fear sits in the outer ring of the circle as an influencer. Fear should *not* invade your inner circle. *Fear is not who you are, who you are is how you address fear.*

I did contemplate whether it was a good idea to share some personal examples of fear. Previously I might have been concerned about what you might think of me but, for me personally, now I don't care. I only care if my sharing causes you to not give the information in this book the same regard. If that happened, it could actually be hampering my intended purpose.

This is where a number of topics in this chapter and my fundamentals and principles come together. I am writing this book with the hope of helping others. My concern does not change that hope, and my reason for sharing is still to help by sharing some real-life experience. I could worry about the lack of acceptance, how that might impact your acceptance of the information, and how that could undermine achieving my desire to help. Those statements would break a couple of guidelines and let that worry into my inner circle. I cannot control what you are going to think and I take responsibility for my sharing. I am sharing with the belief and *intent* of helping. I have no information that makes me believe that it will have a negative impact. The scenario described has multiple layers of *ifs*, for which I cannot be responsible. Worry and fear can get complicated fast. The result of this is that I will share and hope it provides some value to your understanding that can be applied to yourself.

I will pick three fears. I have a fear of heights, I am claustrophobic, and I have had panic attacks that started unrelated to those two fears. Look at all the opportunity I had to address fear.

Let's start with the most acute, panic attacks. I had no signs or indications that I would have a panic attack or that I was having one until I was in the hospital. As I look at what led up to it, it is probably pretty clear but I had no thought of it at the time. I had been working

Part 2: Life's Realities

80+ hour weeks for about 3 months straight. I would drink about 3 pots of coffee and a six-pack of cola every day. Trouble. I was driving my hour and half daily drive home in the wee hours of the morning when it hit me. I thought I was having a heart attack. I had a hard time breathing, chest pressure, and felt as though I was going to pass out. Horrible anytime but I was driving. I managed to pull off the road and call 911. After an ambulance ride to the hospital and discovering that my heart rate was over 200, they gave me nitro. Since it turned out to not be a heart attack, my blood pressure or heart rate went really low after the nitro. Lots of tests later, the presumption was that it was a panic attack. Since there is no test for a panic, it was a presumption but I believe a very valid one based on the circumstances.

The panic attack was certainly fear when it was happening but prior to when it hit I don't think I was afraid of anything; I *was* stressed to the max. I had clearly abused my body and it impacted my mental state, which in turn impacted my physical state. I will not go through the years that I spent addressing the panic attacks once it started but the short story is that once they started, it was difficult to stop them. I tried medication, therapy, meditation, and anything that seemed like it might work. Medication did nothing for me. The combination of therapy and meditation gave me some skills to address the symptoms in order to "suppress" the panic. The time between episodes got longer and the severity of an episode was able to be under control. I abruptly stopped coffee, all other caffeinated drinks, and chocolate and ended up with withdrawal headaches but they went away after a few weeks. That was about 25 years ago and I still don't drink coffee.

The fear of heights has been with me as far as I can tell for the vast majority of my life. I just avoid heights. Even though it has caused some impactful decisions in my life it is probably the least impactful of the three fears that I am talking about. If I had to climb a ladder higher than one story, I would hire someone. There are most always different paths to take when walking along the edge of high places. I remember taking a tour of a massive cargo ship. While with this small tour group inside the ship, we came to a spot where there was a catwalk across the cargo hold that was probably 25 feet up in the air. No way! I told the tour guide that I was going back. The tour path was not marked nor was it intended to be walked in the reverse direction and it was dark, but it was better than crossing that catwalk. It really was not a big deal for me and I didn't think too much about the decision. I have never had a desire for a job that would put me high in the air like roofing, washing windows, iron worker, etc. so the issues with heights is just an adaptation for me. People that see my avoidance can sometimes be cruel and make fun of me but big deal. That is their issue not mine.

If the escalator was multi-story and the were no walls so it was open down multiple stories, the answer would be to take the elevator and that's where the bigger impact of fear was that needed to be addressed. Elevators – claustrophobia.

My claustrophobia certainly escalated after the panic attacks started. The increased fear of closed spaces was due to the concern it would trigger a panic attack and that made the avoidance more pronounced. I would avoid elevators and, before I got it under control, I turned down jobs because of the floor they were on in a building; too high in the building and couldn't take the stairs. I turned down opportunities for jobs and activities that involved air travel (that was the claustrophobia not the heights). The short story on this is that group therapy and meditation helped a great deal. One of the most pronounced impacts of group therapy was getting partnered with a person that had a fear of open spaces. She would ride with me in the elevator and I would walk with her in the open parking lot. It might seem silly but it helped a great deal. I now take elevators on a regular basis, sometimes with a little anxiety, and air travel is not an issue. An MRI is still an issue.

Part 2: Life's Realities

I have shared a few pages of details about my personal fears, so I want to explain why. It is not something that I needed to do for me at this point. I do understand that fear is real. It may be that you think that my examples are extreme or minor compared to yours. The perception of impact is unique and personal. Regardless of the severity, most people, if not all people, have some sort of fear and/or worry that impacts their life. Most people don't talk about them for fear of embarrassment, judgment, or that it is just personal and nobody's business. It is also likely that many people think that they are alone in their fears. Clearly they are not, but even that is not the most important point.

Why spend so much time on fear? As stated, fear is an influencer that sits in the outer ring of the circle but there are many influencers. Why so much focus on this one? It has also been stated that it is not, or should not be, part of your inner core where self-esteem and inner peace live. This "external" influencer is very unique and therefore needs special attention. All of the types of fear used as examples, as well as general worries and fear of fear, come from within. They come from within and yet they sit in the outer circle that is labeled *external influencers*. How are they external if they come from within?

The circle is the fundamental process. Fears and worries sit outside of your fundamentals, so they are external to the fundamentals. It is learning that comes from fears filtered through the fundamentals just like other influences. They build knowledge and are used to find patterns. They update your inner core. Process-wise, they are very much external. The extra risk with them coming from within is that they can attack your inner core directly if you let them.

Fear is a strong opponent and prevailing over fear brings great rewards. Your fabric and the fundamental process is your defense against fear.

Franklin D. Roosevelt said, "courage is not the absence of fear, but rather the assessment that something else is more important than fear."[42]

Again, fear is not who you are, who you are is how you address fear.

Chapter 2-22
PAIN

Whether physical or emotional, pain can be disruptive. Reason, logic, and knowledge can be overshadowed and your fundamentals can be challenged. People deal with pain in many different ways. Mind over matter has an opportunity to be applied. Pain is a true test of the accuracy and strength of your fundamentals and principles. It is not so much that they will make the pain go away but rather a question of whether they withstand the pain. This is not a statement that discards or diminishes the power and reality of pain.

Let's try to put some *perspective* on pain. Pain is certainly subjective and it is a good word to apply relativity. There are so many circumstances that factor into pain; the context of the pain and history leading up to the pain are both relevant. It is extremely unlikely that any given pain is identical from one person to another. There are certainly similarities but uniqueness always exists.

Because of the uniqueness of pain, the statement of "I know how you feel" or even "I can imagine how you are feeling" are both irritating to me. They might be irritating to many and some maybe accept them as just caring interactions, which might be precisely how they are intended. This applies to both physical and emotional pain and it is more than "everything is relative".

Doctors will ask you to rate your pain between 1 and 10. If it is the worst pain you have experienced it is probably close to a 10 if not a 10. That "same" pain may be experienced by someone else and be rated a 3 because of their previous experiences and the context in which it is applied. That is why the only relevant use of that pain level information is relative to different times from the same person.

The impact of pain on your decisions can be immense. Apply the simple and awful concept of torture. Torture is used because it works and it can change people's decisions as well as the course of people's lives. As with many things, this can be used as manipulation but most pain does not exist for the purpose of manipulation. It does however alter your decisions, your mind, your priorities, and it will truly test your foundation. Talking about extremes of pain are easy examples to use but there is not a black and white cut off point where it impacts and it doesn't impact. Pain can be very gradient in its impact. In your conscious implementation of your fundamentals, it is one of the things to be aware of as being an external influencer. Not all pain may be *recognized* as influencing your decisions and potentially having a long-term impact on your fundamentals.

Even for the same person, pain reactions and responses can be very different and there is something more to it than just pain threshold. I shot a nail through my finger with a nail gun and calmly drove to the ER to get it removed. It wasn't that bad. I cut the tip of my finger off with a razor blade. I wrapped my bleeding finger in a towel and took the tip of my finger to the ER to get reattached. It wasn't that bad. My knee got ripped out of place and my foot was facing backwards when I was 16 and my mom drove me to a chiropractor to get it *cracked* back into place. That one hurt quite a bit but consider the conditioning that I got from my parents. My dad stuck a hot needle through my fingernail that had been slammed in a car door to relieve the pressure. The relief felt far better than the pain of the needle going through my fingernail. All of these stories don't make me tough or a person with a high threshold of pain. I can hardly stand to walk barefoot unless it is a beach with no rocks or shells or grass with no rocks or sticks. The point is that there is far more to pain than just physically being hurt.

As stated earlier, the pain can be either physical or emotional, and many times it is both. Since emotional pain can cause physical symptoms and physical pain can cause emotional distress, there is probably little reason to spend a lot of time separating the two of them. The characteristics of how they may grow or heal is certainly different but unchecked pain will impact your state of mind, your decisions, and your fundamentals regardless of the type of pain. It is not true however that the cause of the pain, or the perceived cause of the pain, does not matter. Your understanding of the cause of the pain and your perception of how it stops are probably the two most critical factors in *how* pain has an impact. The pain itself may make it hard to think or concentrate, but the thoughts and conclusions are very much driven by these two perceptions.

I have met a few people that just seem to ignore pain. They don't seem to think about it, make determinations as to its source, or make conclusions on how devastating or debilitating it might be. The people that stand out to me in this category are generally quite old (80s and 90s) and seem to be in very good shape or at least are very active for their age. There is probably something to that. Their pain is maybe no less intense for them than others and I have no idea of their physical threshold of pain, but there is something in them than just accepts and moves on. There is a good chance that they have been that way for a lifetime. This does not mean that you should never go to the doctor or ignore all pain, but their ability to accept reality, adjust, and not internally debate the potential sources, reasons, and outcomes of the pain allows them to continue to be who they are and live their consistent fundamentals.

People like this are *not* the most common, so for the rest of the population pain will have more impactful reactions that can alter the course of your fundamentals, principles and ultimately your decisions. If you are conscious of the pain and the way it impacts you, it can become just one of the considerations for prioritization.

Avoidance of pain can be a powerful motivator as well. Remember this is both physical and emotional/mental pain. If something "hurts", one way to address it is to avoid it. Consequently the more things that hurt you, the more you have to potentially avoid. Keep in mind many of the decisions impacted by pain may not be conscious decisions. This is a good reason for a reminder that being aware of yourself, your external influencers, and your fundamentals is the power that can lessen the *impact* of pain.

Chapter 2-23
HATE

Is hate the opposite of love? On the surface it might seem so but I don't think so. Does hate require passion? Does hate have as many use cases as love? Is hate useful? We could go on with the questions but let's talk about some answers.

The first step in most topics of this book is to look at the definition. While we have not always done that, it is important in this case. Merriam-Webster's sample definitions of hate are as follows:

hate: (noun): *"1 a: intense hostility and aversion usually deriving from fear, anger, or sense of injury..."* [43]

hate: (verb): *"1 a: to feel extreme enmity toward : to regard with active hostility..."* [44]

These are just the first in each category but provide enough to discuss. The noun definition acknowledges some potential sources of hate but uses the word "usually" preceding the list of sources making the source or cause somewhat irrelevant. The verb definition refers to enmity whose definition refers to active hatred. (Another circular definition that is of little value). Where does that leave us? The common sentiment across both the noun and the verb is that it is intense, extreme, active and hostile. That is enough to provide a baseline for the definition.

With that definition in mind, is it the opposite of love? Our resulting fundamental definition of love required action but it is not extreme in the opposite direction, nor does it require the opposite of hostile. What it does have in common with love is that it is very overused. "I hate broccoli." I don't think that fits the literal definition so let's try to stick to the literal for ease of discussion.

The word extreme implies beyond normal and I would say likely beyond control. It is hostile, which creates an opposition and an enemy by its nature. When you combine the two of those things, it is likely that everything surrounding hate becomes blinded. There is a reason for the term blind rage but we are not talking about rage, although hatred can certainly lead to rage. Hate, itself, can be blinding enough.

By the definition of hate being an intense and extreme emotion of hostility toward an enemy, do you think that you can hear anything positive about that enemy, or hear anything *from* that enemy? This book has been about defining yourself and making consistent decisions based on you. How is that possible when you are blinded? I will answer that one; it is not. People make irrational decisions that are outside of themselves when they are based on hatred. Someone might say that they don't let hatred interfere with rationality. I don't believe that is possible. It will always be, at a minimum, a factor of a decision, and because of its intensity it will dominate the decision to the degree that you allow. You are probably getting this chapter's perspective on hate.

As with all other aspects of life, you cannot control the world. You only have your own accountability. Also, consistent with other aspects of life, it is beneficial to be aware of the world around you and that hatred does exist. You can *choose* how you address it both within yourself and from external sources. We will never eliminate hatred in the world, just like we will never eliminate other negative aspects of life. That does not mean that we give in, give up, or feel doomed. We can have hope; not the hope of eliminating hate but the hope of lessening its impact on ourselves and others. You may decide that a particular conversation is lost and walk away from it and *that* is not losing. It is recognition of the context and a willingness to be true to yourself.

We are not here to diagnose the minds of the people that hate. The existence of hate is real and how we address it takes strength. This strength is not a response with more hatred but rather strength of personal responsibility to your own fundamentals and principles.

Chapter 2-24
DEATH

It would be remiss to spend an entire book discussing so many aspects of life and not even mention death. Life and death are uniquely tied together. I mentioned the Ben Franklin quote in the chapter on learning, "nothing can be said to be certain, except death and taxes." [45] It was pointed out that not everybody pays taxes; we will all die.

If you were thinking that the chapter on death would be about what happens during or after death, it is not. Since those aspects of death fall to believing and faith, we will leave that to your fundamentals. We also cannot address *why* people die or why they die when they do. It may seem cold but as stated in a chapter on equality, life is not fair and expectations of the most basic things, such a living, can be disappointing.

There are many ways to talk about death. There is the concept of friends and family dying and the devastating sorrow that can bring. There is the overwhelming fear of death and how that fear can rule one's life. There are those that believe that death is a new beginning and not the end. There are murders, accidents, and illnesses that take lives.

There is also the aspect of death that includes suicide, which I want to separate from all of the others.

Suicide is not something that I should, can, or will address other than recognizing its existence. I do not understand it and I would do anything I could to prevent it and help those that feel whatever it is they feel that takes them to that point. I am helpless in that regard other than being a person willing to share what I can and be there for anyone that reaches out. I am also not going to address the aspect of murder from the killer's perspective; another perspective that I have no experience or rational deduction that can be applied other than there are people that are not only willing to kill but get some level of satisfaction from killing others.

The remainder of the examples fall into a category of unexpected, although maybe not immediate, death with two subcategories of yours and others. This may seem ridiculously simplistic but, again, simple is one of the keys to consistency and value. In addition to the obvious difference between the two, there is the fact that immediate unexpected death only applies to others. Your own death can be immediate but it is one of those scenarios that isn't irrelevant to this purpose. After all, your immediate death would have no impact on your foundational or tuning priorities or the decisions you will make in the future. It may have impact on others, but that would be the other subcategory.

Of the two subcategories, your impending death is the one that we will spend the majority of time on. It would be good if the accidental or impending death of others would have the same impact, and it is possible, but it is rare. I have lost *all* of my immediate family members and many friends and acquaintances and only one of them had the type of impact as my own impending death. Even that one was after my own impending death experience so I cannot state whether the impact would have been the same.

I did some general searching for common feelings when you lose a friend and when you are told that you are terminally ill. According to the "Internet", the feelings are pretty much the same. I can tell you that for me they were not at all the same. I am guessing that those Internet conclusions were reached by what people *think* should be the reactions or presume would be. I am also not going to presume that everybody reacts the way I have because I know that is not true. Both can generate sadness and anger but they are not the same. One of the comments about the impact of the death of a friend was assessment of your own mortality. It is doubtful that the assessment is the same for anyone. There is a big difference between the thought of "that could be me (sometime)" and "I have months to live." From my perspective, it is about as different as sitting in your living room in Minnesota and watching the report of a hurricane in Louisiana, and hiding in your basement while a tornado is ripping your house apart above you.

A very appropriate quote at this point comes from Mahatma Gandhi, "Live as if you were to die tomorrow. Learn as if you were to live forever." [46] This has become one of my favorite quotes. This is *life* in the context of death. This is appreciating what you have and always thirsting to learn. This is not a focus on death but a realization as well as when and how to address it in your life. A few times in my life I have believed that there was a reality facing me that my life would be ending soon. That was certainly not something that I wanted and not something that I could say that I embraced, but rather accepted as a probable reality and my focus shifted toward how to live. It is very revealing what people will choose when faced with this situation. I do not wish this on anyone, but I do wish the results on everyone.

It is very cliché, but most people find what has been stated over and over; the important things cannot be bought. The stuff that you have, the new car, the bigger house, and the designer clothes make absolutely no difference. People will look for love, safety, comfort, the meaning of life, purpose, their soul, their spiritual nature and relationships. How many people that have never prayed, start praying? How many people make phone calls that have not been made for years or change their behavior and purpose in what they believe to be their last days?

The Gandhi quote addresses this concept entirely. It is very difficult for many however to know what it means to them until they face it. I wish that I had a way to make that happen and I continue to hope and try by writing things like this. Maybe one person will make that leap. This sentiment has been expressed in various ways throughout this book. The way you find your foundation, how you implement it, and the way you tune your priorities can all be attributed to this way of thinking. It is what finding the *important* decisions is all about. Everything that you learn enhances your understanding and your ability to tune your foundation and execute your life against that foundation that brings a peace of mind that cannot adequately be described in words.

This chapter started with the statement that life and death are uniquely tied. As you can see, the majority of the discussion regarding this topic of death was about how to live. Acknowledging the inevitability of death enhances living.

Chapter 2-25
PRIORITIES

I want to point out that priorities are *not* your principles and not your fundamentals. Priorities are the way that you rank your principles and the *important* things in your life. Remember the discussion of important decisions? The noise should have already been eliminated before applying prioritization. There is no reason to prioritize noise.

Another important aspect to remember is that priorities can be contextual. It is good to find the breakpoint where context does not have an impact. There may always be rare exceptions but there are likely a *few* priorities that you have that would be unlikely to be compromised by context. A few examples might be family over acquaintances, health over money, and integrity over acceptance. Most, however, are contextual so storing the reusability of the priorities becomes challenging. This is where patterns are very helpful. It is also valuable to look at priorities being contextually driven by your fundamentals. This might seem out of place if you remember that there can be no conflict between fundamentals and principles, however this does not dispute nor conflict with that. Your fundamentals, as in your fabric, allow for the contextual flexibility to apply them when needed to aid in prioritization.

We all make prioritization decisions every day and almost every moment of every day. It is a far better practice to make strategic decisions rather than impulsive ones. If you start at the highest level of priorities, the lower priority-level decisions that happen more frequently will be easier if you can get in the practice of recalling your strategic decisions. Another way of putting that is that it is hard to make appropriate decisions if you don't know what direction you want to go.

One of the easiest examples to use is money. The reason for that is that a financial budget is a list of priorities. One thing that priorities have over a budget is that there are no "rich" people when it comes to priorities. Some people have so much money that a budget, as most people know it, is irrelevant because they will not likely ever reach the bottom of their resources. The resource that everyone has in common is time. We all have 24 hours in a day.

When you create a budget based on your available resources, you will allocate funds to bills, to food, to medical, and other areas that fall into a category of *need*. Then *if* resources allow, you will allocate money to savings and money to entertainment, to charities, or money toward supporting or enriching others. If you know your priorities, it doesn't mean that you can't change them based on context but it sets guiderails to *help* prevent totally impulsive decisions.

There are so many ways to spend money. If you pretend that you have unlimited resources when you don't, you will run out of resources and find that you have spent money on things that were not your highest priorities such as food to feed your family. When you run out of resources, you are left with fewer options to solve the situation. You could get another job, but that would likely limit some of your other priorities. You could get a loan or use a credit card, but doing that would reduce your future resources that have already run short.

Part 2: Life's Realities

When you get out of this scenario of a financial budget and move on to the much more important and complex budget of time, there is no option to add to your resources by getting a loan. When it is gone, it is gone. When you find that there is no time left to do the more important things, you may realize or think that you forgot to prioritize. Actually, you did prioritize; you probably just did it "wrong". It is wrong because you identify what is important and if you did not execute to what *you* defined, either your definition or your execution was wrong. This could be an example of where the execution of your priorities, and potentially principles and fundamentals, have failed.

These failures can be based on not knowing your priorities or needing to modify them, but it is likely more often driven by impulse; the bird in the hand syndrome. These examples of priorities are worthy of consideration for a principle. With the appropriate principles and the honor to hold to them, the number of "failings" *should* be reduced. Impulse can be strong, so there is no expectation of 100% compliance.

We were initially talking about the on-the-fly decision prioritizations and we should get back to that. On-the-fly is very often, barring any other methodology, a "go with your gut" response. It is likely that everybody has an idea of what that means, but where does that gut feeling come from? We talked about building your inner core and the automated subconscious actions that can come from that place; your "gut" is the same place. As complex as the contextual prioritizations can be to store for reuse, this gut feeling becomes that fallback when there is not a specific rule or condition available. We talked about the fact that the inner core exists and self-esteem, self-respect, and inner peace reside there. This idea of a gut feeling brings another angle to the importance of nurturing your inner core. The process of filtering noise and adding your guidelines through your fundamentals, in order to build knowledge and patterns, is clearly important to making your inner core align with you.

This is where you might be able to see how a negative impact that gets through to your inner core could be very disruptive going forward. Take the time to nurture your inner core and check it once in a while against your principles and fundamentals to make sure that your gut reactions are in sync. With this concept in mind, the phrase of "go with your gut" is *not* just a random or off-the-cuff non-caring solution; it is you.

Part 2: Life's Realities

Chapter 2-26
THE SELF-THINGS

What are the self-things? This chapter was going to be only about self-esteem, which will still be a big part of the focus, but it expanded quickly into self-respect and then to self-confidence. While there are some differences between them, the commonality is very important and it is hard to talk about one without talking about the others.

I would like to say that this is easy but as you probably know, everything is simple and nothing is simple. The simple part of this is that if you know your fundamentals and live by them, it will inherently promote self-esteem. Basing self-esteem on your fundamentals removes the tendency to combine or confuse self-esteem with pride in your talents or, even worse, letting it be driven by others' opinions of you and their definition of success and value. This may not even be their definition but your *perception* of their definition.

Those that have low self-esteem may not have recognized the importance of their fundamentals and living them. How can you not be proud of love, hope, your beliefs and honor? Any one of those are admirable but when combined and understood to be your foundation, knowing that you live your life by those has so much power to impact others and the entire world. How can you not be proud of who you are?

I have used the word proud or pride a couple of times now in this chapter and I have been avoiding that word up until now. Why now? We better look at the definitions in Merriam-Webster's Dictionary:

> **pride:** "*1 a: inordinate self-esteem : CONCEIT   b: a reasonable or justifiable self-respect...*" [47]

The first definition is the reason I have avoided the use of the word. The second definition is the reason that I am using it now. It does, however, bring up another related definition question.

What is the difference between self-esteem and self-respect? Checking Merriam-Webster's Dictionary for both:

> **self-esteem:** "*1: a confidence and satisfaction in oneself : SELF-RESPECT...*" [48]
>
> **self-respect:** "*1: a proper respect for oneself as a human being...*" [49]

The definition of self-respect does not help clarify the answer to the question, but two of the synonyms listed for self-respect are pride and self-esteem. It would seem the question is answered. The two words point to each other. While there are debatable nuances between self-esteem and self-respect, we will consider that this chapter can encompass both in the same discussion. I will offer that the difference is *probably* similar to the relationship between responsibility and accountability in that one might generally be before and the other after. Let me explain. The chapter on respect referenced trust. This chapter relates the trust in self-respect as equating to believing that you *will* do the right thing. Self-esteem may be more about pride in that you *have done* the right thing. I will emphasize again that this pride is *not* conceit.

It has been discussed, and likely will be again, that the impact of events on other people will never be known. There is nothing in the fundamentals or in the execution of the fundamentals that should indicate your purpose is to make others see you in a good light or think of you as successful. What *is* mentioned is the context of trust and the perception of others related to your consistency. When your consistency is based on your fundamentals, there is a position of integrity that would be difficult for anyone, especially yourself, to challenge in any logical or meaningful way.

So what does integrity have to do with self-esteem? I would say everything, but it is a little more complex than a one-to-one relationship. If people know what to expect of *you*, they depend on those expectations and their reliance on those expectations changes their actions and decisions. You may never see or hear of most of them. If that consistency is based on your fundamentals, *there is inevitable positive impact on others*. If you are widely, consistently, and positively impacting others, what reason is there to not be gratified and filled with self-esteem?

Self-esteem is not conceit, it is not success as defined by others, it is not dependent on others at all; it is yours to earn and you own the qualifications. The qualifications are your own internal alignment to your fundamentals. This can be very difficult for some and some may challenge that they do not "deserve" their own self-respect and self-esteem. I am not going to restate my comments (on deserve) that are made in the chapters on expectations and equality, but the word is not in my normal vocabulary. It is only used here in the context of what someone else might say or think.

There are so many words associated with self-esteem which makes it a very pervasive part of your life. Some of them are confidence, appreciation, worth, value, pride (the right one), trust, and respect to name a few. They all have one thing in common from the perspective of this chapter; they are all inward and owned by you. There is *no* external dependency on any of these terms and concepts.

Using self-worth as one of the examples, I want to point out that *feeling* value is far different and far more important than someone's recognition of your value. Recognition feels good, but for too many those two are tied or are even seen as synonymous. Similarly, doing for others is different than pleasing others. It is so important that *you* recognize what you are doing in order to tune and clarify your fundamentals, and if you are focused on your fundamentals you will have the tools to recognize your actions.

I am hoping that this is not coming across as saying, "In order to be happy, just be happy" equating to, "In order to have self-esteem, appreciate yourself." While that is not a misrepresentation, it is not a snap of the fingers. It is recognized that some people are shy and lack confidence in themselves and overcoming that may be very difficult. It is also recognized that the reason people may feel that way can vary greatly. So what is the purpose of all of this?

You do not have to be the most talented person, the most successful person, the outgoing person, or any of the descriptors commonly put on people that are *perceived* to have confidence in themselves. You just need to believe in your fundamentals. Since believing is one of the fundamentals, if you have fundamentals defined and a commitment to them, you are there. Self-confidence like all of the other self-things, is self (internal) driven. However, it is one that also has a significant outward-facing perception. It is a *perception*, which is important to remember. You providing the basis for the perception to others is the only way they will perceive it. In their perception, they will likely have no idea what is internal to you, such as why or how, but they can see a what.

This is not encouraging deception or making others' perceptions a goal. This is recognizing the reality of others in your life and the negative influence those things like acceptance, rejection, and embarrassment can have on your self-anything. I was very shy and quiet. In fact my nickname in college was mouse, and yet I ended up in a band playing in front of thousands of people. I also ended up liking to speak in front of large crowds. I am not going to go through the whole progression that took me there, but I was doing something that I wanted to and not doing it would have not been true to myself. Regarding the fear of people "judging" me, many times people see confidence more than talent. That is not to say that talent and skills are not important or worthy of self-respect. Let me give you a couple of examples.

Imagine a doctor walking into the examining room after a series of tests and saying "Well, I studied something like this in school, but I didn't really understand it very well. I think that this might be that same thing so, if you're okay with it, let's try a couple of medications and see if it helps." Some may say that at least they were honest and they would like that, but imagine a different communication. "This looks like xyz and the treatment for that is these two medications. This should clear up within 10 days, but if it gets worse or doesn't get better, call me." Both conversations were with the same person with the same talents and neither one was a lie. Which one instills confidence and makes you think the doctor is a "better" doctor?

Here's one more lighter example. In this case, I will make the talents very different. The more talented of two musicians walks out on stage and says "I have been practicing this song for a couple months and it is really a struggle. I want to try and play it for you. Please forgive me if I make too many mistakes." The musician sits down on a chair and starts to play an extremely difficult piece and makes two very small mistakes. The other musician walks out to the front of the stage and yells "HOW'S EVERYBODY DOING? EVERYBODY UP ON YOUR FEET AND LET'S GET THIS PARTY STARTED!" They stay at the front of the stage, kick their foot, and start to play a very simple song. I am not saying that talent doesn't matter and people can't appreciate talent, but many people would appreciate the second musician more.

Again, this is not suggesting that you lie to people or yourself but rather the opposite. Be true to yourself and believe in yourself, and your confidence is what people will see. Grab hold and enjoy the joy, freedom, and inner peace that comes from that.

The self-things are not something that someone can give to you; you give them to yourself.

Part 2: Life's Realities

Chapter 2-27
MAKING DECISIONS

We have talked a lot about decisions. We just talked about *going with your gut* related to contextual priorities. The beginning premise of creating fundamentals was to make decisions. You might even say that this whole book is about making decisions. Decisions are pretty much the way we live. Everything we do is a decision unless you believe in predetermination, in which case I am not sure why you would be reading this book. Making a decision implies the belief in free will. We can choose and we choose every minute of every day. Most of the decisions, of course, are minor but every decision can impact your life as well as someone else's.

We do let our decisions run on autopilot for most minor decisions, which is just fine as long as we check the autopilot once in a while to verify that it is still working to specifications.

Decisions are your crossroads. Some people may equate crossroads with making a deal with the devil and the story of Robert Johnson, but maybe only guitar players know that story. I am referring to crossroads as every decision that you make. There is no option to not make a decision because no decision is a decision. Every day you will make multiple decisions (maybe hundreds); some are big and many are small. Some decisions are planned and strategized, some are thrust upon you, and some are behavior or autopilot decisions. I recently made plans to retire and made a very conscious decision with a roadmap to retire. I use the word retire very loosely but that is irrelevant to this point. I planned a change in my life and in my source of income. At the same time, I received a medical diagnosis that modified my long-term plans and gave me a lot more decisions to make.

Decisions and the concept of crossroads are seldom binary, as in they are not just left or right or yes or no. There are variants of every decision and you may even decide to not take a predefined road. I ran across a desk sign some time ago and I bought two of them, one for one of my children (why only one I don't know), and one that I kept for myself. It simply says, " Life is all about how you handle plan B". That is so, so true. Part of making a decision is the recognition that you may have to reassess your decision when the circumstances change or when the outcome isn't as planned. That is absolutely critical. If that is not accepted, if not assumed up front, you will risk making a decision that you really did not want to make, or you will get very frustrated or depressed that things are not going as you planned.

Certainly applicable to decisions, as well as life in general, is a quote from Heraclitus, "there is nothing permanent except change." [50] This is a quote from around 500 BC and it is still very relevant. The quote is used with a caveat that I found at least four variations of this quote which is not too much of a surprise being from 500 BC and everything changes. This quote is used with a bit of concern because, while it is inevitable that change will happen and decisions will need to be assessed, you own your own *internal* consistency. Your foundation can be consistent regardless of the inconsistencies that happen around you.

Part 2: Life's Realities

Decisions are inevitable and you are *forced* to make them because, again, no decision *is* a decision. Do you feel pressure or even stress being told that you are *forced* to do something? That stress is also a decision, believe it or not. As you become more grounded in your fundamentals and principles, the decisions become faster and easier to the point where many are subconscious reflexes. This does not mean that all easy decisions are reactions to things that happen. Decisions can be both planful as well as reactive. The decisions that you make start blending into to a *behavior for which you are recognized*.

The purpose of your decisions is not for the recognition, but rather for the alignment with your fundamentals. Everything flows from that. If the purpose shifts to recognition, the execution of your fundamentals becomes corrupt because fundamentals are actions and events and they do not guarantee results. Some of these statements have been made previously in variations throughout this book, which is not a surprise since we have already stated that this book is arguably about decisions.

So what is the point of making decisions? Or what is the point at all? We decide what to wear, when to eat, what to eat, what route to take, and as you move into things that are much more impactful, what to say, what to do, and how to feel. Yes, we decide it all. So, I get to decide how I feel? Yes. Nobody said that you would be successful, or that there will not be major forces making you believe that you have no choice, but you have more choices than you probably think. All decisions have consequences. No decisions have guaranteed outcomes based on the definition of a fact. There are no future facts, so you make your decisions based on probabilities and beliefs. This is one of the reasons that, for me, believing has to be one of the fundamentals or I would lose the basis for many decisions. Decisions have some level of intent or desire for outcome and outcome is in the future. The future is probabilities and beliefs; therefore decision *expectations* are based on probabilities and beliefs.

Chapter 2-28
REACTIONARY TRIGGERS

A significant amount of decisions and events are reactionary. Some might even argue that everything is reactionary. In the sense that people will consider the context of the situation, it is evident that everything has reactionary impacts, but for the purpose of this discussion we will look at reactions as being the trigger for decisions and events rather than the context. However, all decisions do not need to be triggered by reactions. Some decisions come from within and are not triggered by an external event.

Many decsions, and especially reactions, can be solely based on emotion. This gets into dangerous territory. Emotions are dangerous? Yes, when emotions are the *only* things driving a reaction or decision. Emotional is not the same as passionate. You can be passionate about a position, a fact, or a principle. Regardless of whether a reaction is emotional or thoughtful, it is possible that it is not an action created by you, but rather a *push* against the event or person. This creates a response that is entirely focused on the action or the creator of the action and only conveys anti-action to that event. When you exert force against an action, it will create another pushback action and so it goes.

There is little value in taking action on "I don't like you" or "you are stupid". It conveys no position or event that can have positive value, create conversation, or give others the opportunity to experience new events that can have a potential positive impact on them and others. The resulting emotional pendulum swings seldom have an opportunity to utilize your foundation, convey it to others, take action on it, or even access it. These types of responses often do not represent what you intend to or want to say or do.

The laws of physics, such as Newton's third law about every action having an equal and opposite reaction, are not intended to apply to people. It would however be helpful to keep in mind that it is possible, if not likely, in every action you take. It is helpful from your own self-awareness, but also as an indicator of what to anticipate, if not expect, in return.

Rather than an equal and opposite, or even escalated, response to an action, using the action to trigger access to your foundation allows for a response that communicates who you are rather than what emotions you may be feeling. This does not mean that emotions are a bad thing. Love is an emotion and people that are passionate about something will persist through hard times so emotions are essential to living. Even negative emotions are a reality of living. Using emotions to provide context to an action or reaction will likely prove much more beneficial than letting the emotion itself be the sole factor in the reaction.

Let's use an example to clarify. Say that there is a position being filled at work and you believe that you have proven yourself to be the best candidate for this position, so you applied for the job. The announcement is made and you did not get the promotion and you know for a fact that the person that got the promotion works less than half the hours that you do, produces less than one quarter of the output as you, and has missed about 20 days of work in the last 2 months. You also know that person is very friendly with the president of the company and is younger than you. What you want is to be treated fairly, but you are convinced that their friendship with the president and your age were both factors in this decision. This is going to sound very familiar to the discussion about equality, but this context is the reaction that follows.

When you hear of the situation and begin to assess the reasons for this action, it is a natural reaction to want to either lash out and/or want to fix the situation now and going forward. You clearly have a choice to make and this is not a binary choice. There are thousands of options, but let's pick a few.

An example of a complete emotional reaction that is only pushback, would be to storm into the office yelling about how unfair it was and what horrible people they were for making that decision. You might even accuse them of illegal behavior and threaten to call the police. Rational? Helpful? Does it achieve your goal? I would hope that you would think not, but those types of reactions happen and you have probably had a complete emotional reaction a time or two in your life; I know I have. It can occasionally even feel good to do it. You might lose a job, or a friend, or get thrown in jail but you were able to vent.

Venting is actually the most likely benefit and purpose of such a reaction. Another way to vent might be more beneficial without the unintended and undesirable consequences. You could go outside and yell. You could write a nasty letter or email (and never send it); I have written *many* of those. You could take a calming approach with deep breathing or meditation.

A second option would be to take all of the things that you know and lay them out in a factual way with the person making the decision, ask them for insight into what their decision making criteria included, and collaborate on a plan for your future and proposed subsequent promotion.

Another option for a reaction might be to take the information as an indicator, likely with other information about the decision makers and the company, that this is not a place that you want to work and commit to finding another job. This is using the event as a knowledge and pattern builder.

There is always the option to do nothing more than just be pissed off, bury any action, and just let the situation eat at you. This will likely change your behavior in a negative way. This is another example where no choice is actually a choice that does have consequences; it always does. This is usually not the best choice.

These choices have been addressed in somewhat of a vacuum and are way oversimplified and that is not the reality of life, however, in a moment of an emotionally triggered reaction, there is the risk of treating them that way. This is where wisdom comes into play, as it always should. What other factors should be part of your reaction/decision? Your fundamentals should always be front and center. If not, the integrity of your fundamentals is at risk

As a further example of the reaction/decision process, decisions will likely be in layers whether we consciously think of it that way or not. The potential layers could look something like this:

1. Do you react or not react?
2. If you react, is it now or later?
3. If it is later, what additional information is needed?
4. Process the information and event for a reaction/decision.

Reacting now is likely to be most emotional, but some situations call for immediate reactions. Tuning and using your fundamentals will help guide you through that rapid process. You may even define a principle along the way. It is much better that you try to find a way to use the event as a trigger to your own position, thoughts, opinions, and perspectives that are reflective of you, rather than offering a simplistic escalation response.

Chapter 2-29
THE PURPOSE OF LIFE

Talk about a loaded topic! I bet you can't wait to see what I will say. Neither can I. I knew that I needed to address this topic because how do you write a book about the fundamentals of life and discuss other major topics of life's realities without acknowledging the purpose of life?

It is an age-old question with many answers from various philosophers. It gives people great anxiety looking for it and pondering it. Is it obvious why people even want to know? Most people want to feel they are not only providing *value*, but also aligning with something *bigger*. There is the sense of belonging, appreciation, satisfaction, achievement, and the big unknown of why am I here. I don't want to make this topic about death, but it is a fact that our life on earth is limited and many will ask the question or make a statement that they need a purpose or their life is not worth living. Pure existence is not enough for most, although it is for some. What is enough may change with age or even potentially from day to day.

Some will look at this topic and think about their *purpose* and think big picture of their existence. Some will think short-term as in their purpose *today*. Those looking at the big picture may look in various places with various expectations. They may look to philosophers, to theologians, to a direct connection with God, to the spirits of the universe or whatever they consider the highest power and most knowing source they can imagine. Some will find answers but many will not and will either continue to search or adopt their own beliefs as their personal philosophy of the meaning of life. The meaning and purpose of life is not something that is going to meet the criteria for how a fact has been defined. It would then, by definition, be a belief.

Those that are looking short-term may have already determined their purpose of existence and, if not, that is the first step. How do you determine what is the purpose of the day without knowing how that fits into the purpose of the big picture? This may sound like a heavy burden that the expectation is that every day's purpose aligns with your purpose of life. That was not the intended point. It is rather that every day should not be decided within the context of that single day, or life overall will be floating and a purpose of life would default to "do whatever you want every day". Maybe that is it for some? That does not mean that *every day* must align with a bigger purpose.

Those looking short-term within that day are likely looking for value, appreciation, and all of the self-things (self-respect, self-esteem, etc.). What makes you say, "This was a productive day"? We have talked about the self-things quite a lot and the context of the purpose of life does not change any of that.

Maybe this is the project management training showing in me, but it really is a basic part of any management training. Whether it is a project or finances or career or any goal that you have, the recommendation is to create a plan. In regard to the purpose of life, it does not mean to create a detailed plan for your entire life. However, just like learning, there are some things that benefit others from a standpoint of understanding. The short story on this is you can't know what step to take if you don't know the direction that you're heading. Where is it that you want to be?

If you have defined your fundamentals, you are well on your way to guardrails for your life's purpose. Remember the criterion for a fundamental was that it is a *why*. Hopefully you see the correlation between why and purpose. The reason that you decide things and the reason that you live are hopefully in alignment. Very much in alignment! In the big picture of purpose, it will align with your beliefs and your fundamentals, or your fundamentals or beliefs are flawed. You will never achieve inner peace if there is misalignment of those concepts.

Let's skip to the punch line and tell you that there is no way that *I* can tell you *your* life's purpose. Don't be too disappointed. Many will tell you that they can, in fact many have said that everyone's purpose is the same. I actually found a "wise man" quote that said just that. Some would say that the only purpose is to survive, that it is to succeed, that it is to be happy, and about anything you can imagine. As this book started, a key question to ask of all of those people with those universal answers is *why*. Some of their positions may even beg the question of how prior to why. We can conclude that for anyone to tell you your purpose is a non-starter. In creating or confirming your fundamentals you have identified your important decisions. From your important decisions you have identified the common denominator of why you make the decisions that you do (or want to). Yes, you have done the work to identify your purpose.

I am not trying to imply that you are all-seeing and know the *intent of the universe*. Any human claiming to know that is speaking of their beliefs and we are back to *you* owning your decisions, what to believe, and what is important to you.

For the moment, let's table *what* the purpose might be and talk about some parameters of a purpose, regardless of what that purpose is.

The degree that people think about this question is going to vary greatly. Some may believe that a purpose must be singular, such as their only purpose is to care for their family. There is nothing wrong with that thought, but there are many things that can happen and what happens when you tie yourself to something that is not tied to your lifespan? What happens when your kids move out or you get divorced? Most will not dwell on things ending and that too is fine, but things do end. These are also examples of why the fundamentals focus on the *why* and not the what or how. Hopefully you see how purpose and importance comes back to *why* and your fundamentals.

Some will identify with a *big* purpose such as saving a life by running into a burning building to save someone or donating an organ to save someone, but what happens when that is over? For some it can lead to despair. Finding yourself with seemingly no purpose in life when, right before that moment, your life felt full and you were not only satisfied, you were proud of yourself and you had actually achieved a big goal. This is a big deal! Some cannot find the motivation to go on without knowing their purpose. This is yet another reason that purpose in life should tie to why, because *why never ends and neither does purpose*.

Only you can know who you are and whether you are living to your fabric. Since your goals are defined by your fabric, living up to who you are becomes your purpose. Considering all that came before in this book, it is far more complex than saying "be yourself". Hopefully that means *far more* to you now than it would have if you had read it in the first paragraph of this book.

Chapter 2-30
SUMMARY THUS FAR

There are a number of one-liners and short quotes that might provide some of the essence of this book but what do you usually do with those? You might read them and say, "yeah that's nice, but then what?" Have you thought about what it really means, the impact of what it means, or how it might actually impact you? Being true to yourself is one of those nice statements and a binary choice but understanding yourself, in order to be *true to yourself*, is the first step. Tuning the understanding is the second, practice in execution is third, and so the circle begins. Understand that in the third step, tuning will continue to happen and wisdom will grow. You have to be aware in order for that to happen or you ramble and wander not knowing where you're going or even who you really are.

This part of the book covered a lot of territory including examples of external influencers, implementation of your fundamentals, and life's realities. As stated, this book is not telling you what decisions to make.

I hope you have a good understanding of *why* that is not the intent of this book.

As stated at the beginning of Part 2, the chapters could be read in a different order and new understandings or ideas would come to mind. Some of the chapters explicitly referenced other chapters but there is more to it than that. It is all part of the circle and *everything* is related in some way. It was also stated that this part of the book would discuss real topics and include my perspective as well as some personal examples. It certainly did that and you may or may not agree with all of my perspectives and that is okay. I do believe, however, that you should have a perspective on these subjects and how they might align with *your* fundamentals.

Throughout this book I have gone to various dictionaries (most of them not used) and have had issues with many of the definitions. I was beginning to question the reliability of dictionaries as a source but it is worthy of further inspection. I have long been a believer that words have meaning (of course) and that *consistent* meaning and appropriate use of words is important. Unfortunately, and somewhat surprisingly, conflicting with that is the need to communicate with others and others do not always have those same beliefs. Some of the issues that I had with some dictionary definitions were technical in the way the definition was conveyed. This included such things as using the word that is being defined in the definition or using another word that, when you look that word up, points back to the original word. I see no value in that circular self-referencing definition but let's set that shortcoming aside.

The more important observation and a learning opportunity from the definitions is that the common usage of the word is frequently disconnected from the dictionary. Society seems to have modified the definition in many cases. This is not the definition shown in an "urban dictionary"; these alternate definitions come out in mainstream usage. Is it the dictionary that has not kept up with society or is it society that has completely ignored or modified the meaning of words to meet its purpose? Maybe both? I understand the world evolves, but how do we communicate if the language changes and the documented definition is not what many people mean?

I have done my best to explain and define the definitions that I am using in the context of the book and have noted that I do not expect you or me to adopt these sole definitions in our daily vocabulary because we need to communicate with others.

There are many negatives in life and some we can control or influence and some we simply cannot. Everyone will have their own perspective of those negatives and how to address them. This is in no way judging perceptions or stating that I can possibly understand everyone's situation; I only offer my perspective. There are some that have medically influenced challenges in addressing negatives and this is not intended to be a replacement for addressing physical and mental health issues with your personal professionals.

This book offers considerations for how negative influences relate to life and the fundamentals expressed in this book. The negative influences, as with the positive, come in varying degrees of importance and intensity. An illness, for example, can be a drippy nose that lasts a couple days or a terminal illness. The impact is obviously extremely different, so generalizing an illness as a negative just does not work. This example also fits within the concept that everything is relative and that people will have priorities within their own personal context. Keeping relativity and priorities in mind and intact during negative influences can be *extremely* difficult. I hope that your *whys* will assist you through those times.

Hopefully the strength of your inner core (the positive side) prevails over the bumps that challenge you. I am not minimizing the intensity of the things that can come up, but they are not your core and should not be allowed to win. That being said, losing some of those battles should not make you feel defeated or as though you have failed. One of the four fundamentals that should not fail is honor. Being true to you, even if it is the recognition of the challenges and the difficulty, can provide some level of grounding that can help a great deal.

Part 1 of this book was primarily a positive outlook on the why's of life while pointing out that it was not a fairy tale perspective on life. Life is not always pleasant and we are not always pleasant. Part 2 may come across as the opposite of that to some because there are a lot of life influencers that are negative realities. The general concept is that understanding them is important and Part 1 provides useful tools for the topics in Part 2. Stating this by the titles of the parts, *The Fundamentals* provide useful tools for *Life's Realities*.

Part 3 will hopefully add even more insight into some situations and how they relate to situations in life. They will be mostly positive and motivational perspectives rather than a focus on things that might get in your way. I think everybody needs a bit of both because that seems to be what happens in life.

Throughout this book we have recognized the reality of the external influencers. They are very real, but they are not where the power, control, peace, and important aspects of life exist, unless *you* allow it. This does not mean that you should become an introvert; far from it. It means that focus on your fundamentals, principles, and priorities are your defense. They not only will defend against the disturbances, they will make many of them more and more irrelevant.

The battle of wits, good and evil, happiness and sadness, right and wrong, as well as fact and perception will continue. The world surrounds us with complexity and inconsistencies. This is exactly why the fundamentals are important. Everybody needs grounding. I believe that everybody needs to believe, to love, to have hope and to know who they are. Who you are is the bundling of all of your fundamentals culminating in your commitment to honor. I understand that these are my whys and it has taken plenty of assessment, filtering, and challenging myself with the tenacity of a two-year-old saying *why*.

Here is yet another reminder that the *whys* are the fundamentals and the influencers are the whats and hows (for the most part). A couple of external influencers were identified in Part 2 that are whys, but ones that would not be healthy fundamentals and are not likely to be the things that you *choose* to be the most important to you.

Your fundamentals? I asked that you continue to read before deciding what your fundamentals might be or if you want to start tracking and tuning with the ones provided in this book. You are far enough into this book now to *begin* that process and decision.

It was pointed out in the beginning of the book and multiple times throughout Part 2 that you can create *your* fundamentals. The framework and process will still apply. The guidelines have also been outlined for creating fundamentals. I do not profess to know what is in your heart and in your history. With the guidelines that are there to help ensure the functioning of the process, I believe that most people's fundamentals will not stray far from the ones I have outlined. Again, others certainly could work within the guidelines and I do not know everything (not even close), and you know things that I do not. Those statements are *true* for *everyone*.

As you look to create your fundamentals, ask yourself what important decisions in your life are not covered by the four fundamentals presented here. If you find any, make sure they are *why* and not what or how. Even if they are a why, can you ask why to them and get even lower to find the common denominator?

Let's not leave Part 2 with the potential sentiment that everything is against you and you must be in a constant fight. I want to reference a word that has not been used yet other than in the context of self-things, *appreciation*. Appreciation falls into one of my principles. It is not a why but it certainly is a how. *Appreciate what you have every day.*

What you have is not specific to the things you "own". It includes your relationships, your abilities, your thoughts, and the things and people around you. Slow down and recognize that you have so much regardless of what it is that you don't have. It is not just a simple glass-half-full mentality. Do you tell people that you care? Do you use the things you have instead of looking for more? Do you share your talents? Do you really appreciate how great life is? Being prepared for challenges is important, but nurturing your inner core that should be on the positive side is more important. You will probably find a lot of appreciation sentiments in Part 3.

One more reminder of Part 1 and Part 2: ***The Fundamentals*** provide useful tools for ***Life's Realities.***

Know you. Take action. Take responsibility. Always learn. Trust yourself. Respect yourself. Be strong. Find your inner peace.

PART 3
Coffee Table

Expands on the Meaning and Background of the Photos

Chapter 3-1
COFFEE TABLE INTRODUCTION

The book titled Coffee Table Philosophy was originally published in 2011. It is a book of cover-to-cover photographs with an inspirational or thought-provoking message attached to each one. It had limited distribution so I want to take this opportunity to share the messages. I will also offer some background of the photographs and draw some relationships to the fundamentals.

The book begins with the statement, "My hope is that this book provides enjoyment and entertainment to those who peruse these pages. My aspiration is that it causes you to think. My dream is that it impacts another life for the better. I have had many thoughts, as we all have. Mine may be more or less profound than any others but as we all have a perspective, it is mine that I have the desire, responsibility, and commitment to share." That is still my sentiment today.

Before getting to the book I want to share the story of the book creation, issues encountered, and the use of fundamentals in that process.

Limited printing and distribution were not solely due to technical issues but there were plenty of issues out of my control (and some in my control). The printer went out of business. They actually sold their business and did not transfer the book data. Finding a new printer that would be both able to produce the quality and do it at a reasonable price, proved to be a significant challenge. When I finally landed on one that would offer the best level of both that I could find, they still had another issue in that they do not offer 'Print on Demand' for that size and shape. That inhibits the ability to make the book widely available.

Why am I sharing my struggles with the book? It is not only relevant to the explanation of why Part 3 exists in this book, but it is another personal example of many of the topics covered thus far. I set a goal and I actually thought it was a goal that met the criterion for "reasonable" so that I could be accountable. I set my goal and expectation based on information provided by others. The first information that I had included the facts that I had actually printed a book of good quality and that the printer had been in business for decades.

I had no way of knowing they would sell their business, not transfer the book data, and the new owner would not print the same book at the same price even if I recreated it; all things out of my control. What I was responsible for was the fact that the first printer did not offer distribution services and I was left to try distributing on my own, which I had no idea how to do. Time to move on and learn. I had not made a distribution plan because my focus was to "publish" the book, which was met. I can say that was a success. I could have played a blame game with myself or let others do that, but I actually succeeded at the first goal that I set. I did not know at the time how complex the next step might be. A lot of what-ifs could be applied but it would serve no purpose. As that goal was met, it was time to set a new goal which included distribution and making my book widely available at a reasonable price.

Part 3: Coffee Table

I started my research (my responsibility). I had objectives of quality photo printing, reasonable pricing (or nobody would buy it), and wide availability. My idea of wide availability was not that it would be stocked in all bookstores but would be *available* in all of the major bookstores. I landed on two companies that are major players and both said they offered the services that would meet these requirements. Along the way, I ruled out a number of companies that missed on one or more aspects or failed when I talked to them about their claims. Both of the remaining companies, as seems standard, offer Print on Demand (POD) in order to make the book widely available. I picked one of the two companies and did a sample run of one book. Do I just run and go based on their claims without seeing it? Of course not, and that was a good thing. The print quality was really bad. I selected premium ink and high-quality paper and yet found that it was nowhere near the quality of the first printing and without that quality, the photos lost so much. That just could not be an option. What I thought was a good selection and one that I took responsibility for had failed, but I still had the second company.

It was time for plan B. I had to reformat for a different printer and when that was done it was sample book time with them. The quality was acceptable and everything else seemed to be in place. The next step was to place the order and set up the distribution. I had priced the printed books and the POD pricing but when it came time to order and pay for a bigger run and the POD distribution, there was a glitch. They actually did not offer POD for the size of my book. It was not noted that POD was limited to specific sizes. When I called them, they even said, "We do that size." What they did not say until pushed was that they only print that size in portrait not landscape. They said, "Just turn the book the other way." Talk about losing trust and respect. My photos are mostly full page and some two-page spreads, not to mention the fact that it is a "coffee table book" which I would expect to be laid out in that fashion.

This is where I am as of today. At least I can get books printed in lots that I have to pay for by the lot, but there is no wide distribution. It is only available, at this point, directly from my website and on social media. I am continuing to look for other distribution options. I have not lost hope.

The point of this long story was not to complain or to try to sell the first book, it is rather another real example of so many topics in this book.

I set *goals* based on what I knew at the time. I claimed *success* for what was mine to claim. I took *responsibility* where I could identify it and *learned* from the experience. I set *expectations* both based on my *knowledge* and on claims made by others. My position on *trust* was further verified that trust should not be inherent in status or title. I allowed for a higher *probability* of *truth* based on reputation and allowed my expectations to be set based on those probabilities. I perceived them to be reasonable probabilities. Any movement toward *respect* for these companies took a couple steps backwards. I accepted what I could and could not *control*. There was a learning and *validation* of actions that implied an effort to manipulate the *perception* of potential clients, driven by *greed*. All companies and their services are not *equal*. I was and still am forced to *prioritize* my objectives; quality is at the top and price is second. I eliminated the option for reasonable price and wide distribution with poor quality, and that decision was easy based on my *principles* and *honor*. I made, and continue to make, *decisions* that align with my *fundamentals*. These books are important to me and, because they are so aligned with my fundamentals, maintaining that focus is part of my *purpose in life* (not the *outcome* but the actions that I take). Throughout these complications I have maintained my *self-respect* and built my *self-esteem* by being true to my fundamentals. This need to share is driven by my fundamentals of **love** and **respect** for others. I **believe** that some things in these books will help others. I maintained the commitment and honor to this belief and this love and through all this I still have **hope** and I will continue to work toward bettering myself and offering assistance to others.

Part 3 of this book is intended to provide information that is in the Coffee Table Philosophy book (without the pictures) to those that may not have access to that book. For those that have it, it will provide a little more background on some of the photographs, some ties to the fundamentals, as well as elaboration on some of the messages.

I will offer a brief description of the photos (not a thousand words) for context as well as reprint the unaltered associated statements. It was intended to truly be a coffee table type book that you could just open to random pages and get something from it. Just the act of taking photographs, captures a moment in time and is the recognition of the wonders that exist around us. This expansion cannot replace that.

It is likely that many of the thoughts and underlying purpose of the pages have been addressed thus far in this book, but some additional comments on the context of the photos may reinforce the meaning and expand on its real applicability. In expanding some of the messages, I will directly tie some of them to this book and answer some of the questions that were posed. There were a fair amount of open-ended questions in the Coffee Table book that were intended to encourage thought. While that is also an intent of this book, some questions will be answered simply by tying it to the information in this book.

In some way, I contemplated whether or not this is actually a good idea. The thoughts in the Coffee Table book were, in most cases, very short and did not need explanation. The benefit of that is that people would add their own context and emotion to the statements and photos and derive meaning for themselves. I do not want to destroy that conclusion but rather offer more information to allow for it to be expanded upon. It may be that your conclusion is deeper or more impactful to you than my original thought and that is very much encouraged and applauded. If you have read the Coffee Table Philosophy book and I state something now that does not align with your previous conclusions, please do not let my comments deteriorate or negatively impact your own thoughts. This supports my belief that the efforts and strengths of multiple people combine to be bigger and better than the offering of either alone. My additional thoughts are simply more contribution for consideration rather than restrictions.

Some topics included in these thoughts can be loaded with emotion and emotion is obviously very personal to each of us. Another example of emotional communication that is left open to interpretation is music. It is very seldom that an artist will share the background or specific meaning of the lyrics because it can have the impact of losing appeal. When the consumer is allowed to interpret for themselves in their own context, it will have broader appeal. There are a number of examples where artists have shared their meaning of the lyrics and it was nothing like many people had perceived it to be. I have no information regarding whether or not that "wrecked" the song for people or if they were able to just move on with their original interpretation. Maybe they found something in the explanation that could even enhance or clarify their own interpretation or conclusion. What it should never do is destroy the consumer's thoughts or ability to make it what they need. You own your thoughts and your conclusions and I am simply providing more information for you to consider.

You may see some redundancy in some of the statements, but I prefer to think of it as consistency. The Coffee Table Philosophy book was written ten years ago and the core messages have not changed. Let's get to the book.

Chapter 3-2
COFFEE TABLE EXPANSION

Hope

Photo: The picture is of a city limits sign of a real town in Minnesota. The sign is well beaten and rusty but it is still strong and serving its purpose.

Statement: It is a real place and even though the elements beat at it, it remains.

How could I possibly pass up this sign alongside the road? This was not a town that I just happened across, it is a town that I went looking for. I had seen the signs for Hope on the freeway many times but never really gave it a thought and never took the exit until a seemingly unrelated event brought Hope to my attention.

I was on my first date with my wife and this in-person meeting was the result of almost a month's worth of emails after connecting via the

Internet. We were having dinner in a very nice restaurant and when the waiter came around to explain the menu and specials, they commented on the fact that they had Hope butter. We asked what Hope butter was and were informed that it was butter from a small town in Minnesota called Hope. This person that I met in person for the first time and I looked at each other and said, "Road trip." That comment added more hope.

Hope, being one of the four fundamentals, has been discussed at length. Hope is something that is strong and persistent and when it is lost it can be devastating.

You Have to Start Somewhere

Photo: The photo is of a highway mile marker sign. It is Highway 1, mile marker 0, and the sign above it says BEGIN.

Statement: You have to start somewhere.

Everything starts somewhere. This highway 1 is in Florida. Looking back at where you were and where "it" started can be a good refresher and learning experience, as well as a satisfying sense of accomplishment, whether it was yesterday or 50 years ago.

While looking back can be beneficial, my initial thought on this page was forward looking. Realize that you can still start many things, but you have to start. It doesn't matter how small, just start. I believe the drive to move forward and start can come from all of the fundamentals: love, hope, honor and believing. This emphasizes the point of honor that recognizes the responsibility to try. Saying that you have hope but sitting back and waiting for something to happen is not really hope. Saying that you love in the various ways that love can exist but taking no step forward is not *actionable* love.

The biggest risk, as mentioned before, can come from a misconstrued viewpoint of believing and faith. If you have faith that something will happen, some will use that as a reason to put the action and results in others' hands and take no responsibility. You owe it to yourself, to others, and to your beliefs to take a step and *start*.

Adventure

Photo: A covered bridge surrounded by fall color trees and you can see the shadow of a person through the tunnel of the bridge.

Statement: Experience a new adventure. It does not have to be extreme. Experience something that you have not before. Find new places, new feelings, new thoughts, new life.

This photo was taken on an adventure that my wife and I took driving through the back roads of New Hampshire in the fall.

Don't be afraid of new adventures. Some are small and some are big but a new experience will always offer learning opportunity, to say nothing of just plain fun. It can offer new perspectives and context to future experiences and conversations that can result in better relationships and better understanding. For some, a new experience can be a fearful experience because it touches on that trigger of fear of the unknown. Again, the size and intensity of the experience does not matter. Expanding your horizons, perspective, and context is important and, taking a lesson from the previous page, you have to start somewhere.

Fundamentals of Life

Love in New York

Photo: A black and white photo of a New York street in Manhattan with the 'Love sculpture' highlighted in red.

Statement: Can you really find love anywhere? What kind of love are you looking for? How many kinds of love are there? Is there only one kind and all the others are misrepresented? I love my child different than my mother, different than my best friend, different than my lover, different than my dog. Is love the same as caring? Does love only exist when there is a willingness to put them before you, or when there is commitment or when it is mutual? Can it have constraints or conditions? How will you know love when you see it? Thousands of people walk past love every day without even noticing that it is there. Love is not called out in big bold red letters that make it undeniably obvious. Many become so used to seeing it that they no longer notice its existence, its meaning, or its value. Keep your eyes and heart open.

This is one of the core fundamentals and of course not limited to New York. Hopefully my perspective of the answer to many of these questions has been addressed in the chapter on love as a fundamental. Your personal answers to these questions are more important than mine, but hopefully my offerings can help you find or clarify your own perspective and build the fundamentals of who you are. Keep your heart, mind, and soul open to love.

Part 3: Coffee Table

Perception

Photo: This is a black and white photo of what appears to be a fountain within a structure containing plants, but the clarity of what it is and where it is becomes blurred by the bright sunlight from the opening behind the fountain and the apparent haze in the air.

Statement: Do you see the darkness and feel surrounded or do you see the light and feel hope? Is your perception your reality or is there a true reality? Yes and yes. Your perception is your reality. Can the true reality change your perception? Maybe it can. But can the true reality be found? In some cases, yes. Knowing the origin of this photo allows me a perception that is probably closer to the real truth than what you have. Do you seek out that knowledge or do you prefer to retain your perception and your truth? The fact is that this photo was taken in a very busy market in the middle of the day in a small town in Mexico. This was a moment in time when there were no people in view. Has your perception changed? What lies beyond the gate; a brightness, hope? The reality of the physical nature is that it was weeds and garbage but the lighting changed the whole perception. Your light, your views, your filters create your image of reality. Those that continue to seek out information to clarify their reality will continue to grow and be enlightened.

This was a long statement and there is a great deal of commentary in this book regarding perception, truth and the idea of relativity. The number of topics in the Coffee Table book only emphasizes the importance and pervasiveness of these concepts on our lives. While the statement in the book might imply that the truth is "better" than perception because it provides opportunity for growth, it is not always the case that it is "better". The word better is such a relative and subjective word that it can be a dangerous word to use. I believe that in the vast majority of cases, truth should be pursued and knowledge only serves to enlighten those that are willing to consume it. On the other hand, finding the reality of a situation that is different than your original perception does not negate the value of your original perception should you find value in it. In the case of this photo, if you perceived a calm and peaceful setting and felt a sense of tranquility, the value of that perception should not be undermined by the reality of garbage and weeds. Both can have value depending on the circumstances.

While you may subscribe to one perception over another, it is important to understand the difference between truth and perception. If you subscribe to the concept that the truth is fact, the truth should not be able to be manipulated. If you allow the lines between truth and perception to blur, they will be at jeopardy of manipulation and even deception.

Look for the Constants

Photo: The photo is of a commercial dock with motorboats on one side and various colors of kayaks leaning against a wall at the end of the dock.

Statement: You will always find differences. There is new and there is old. There is color and there is black and white. There is gas powered and man powered, loud and quiet. Where you find the commonality you find an ability to share and communicate. It may open the passageway to new worlds. One constant is water. What constants do you find in your life? They are good indications of your core, your values and the things that are most important to you. They will seldom, if ever, change. This is your foundation.

Do you recognize the substance of the *fundamentals* in this statement? This is conceptually the process of defining fundamentals but without the constraints of the guidelines such as *why*. Look around and see the differences, but the commonality is obvious if you are open to it. By examining that at a deeper level, it is possible that you may find constants that you feel are not how you wish to see your principles and your core. This is good opportunity for self-examination and assessment.

The photo is from New Hampshire. This photo initially struck me as having a high level of contrast. Black and white, color, gas-powered and man-powered and the idea of all the kayaks sitting on the dock with gas pumps. The realization of commonality was also quite obvious. All uses of the area and that dock provide for fun, relaxation and being on the water. This is about being open minded, observing reality, and trying to understand others' perspectives. It refers to finding common ground. This type of thought process is usually thought of in the context of finding compromise. I believe that it is far more fundamental and broader usage than just compromise. In fact, common ground often does not require compromise. Common ground results in better understanding, collaboration, and often times, putting aside the superficial that might be irrelevant to the situation.

Appreciation

Photo: In the midst of a tropical storm with a strong wind blowing at the palm trees.

Statement: After a storm or after the hardships in your life, you often feel more appreciative for the things that really matter. Loss of your house or a loved one or a personal brush with death has a way of making the things that are important rise to the top. I wish that people did not have to experience such hardship to appreciate the things that, with that knowledge, become so obvious. With or without the hardship, I hope that you will find your higher meaning of life, lose any bitterness, and live for today, for tomorrow may never come. Some may see this as a fatalistic view of life, but I see it as an uplifting and energizing view that instills appreciation. I have today and today is a wonder unto itself.

Hardship does change a perspective. Maybe it just makes it easier to see the underlying fundamentals rather than change a perspective. It really is another opportunity for self-assessment. I do not say this lightly. As I reread this statement, it is very clear to me that I write this from a number of personal experiences. This photo is not life and death but the concept can still apply. The palm trees in the photo that can barely be seen for the wind and the rain will take on a different perspective after the storm, with the sun shining and the ocean in the background. Don't forget to appreciate it when the sun is shining.

Music

Photo: A somewhat unique perspective of one of my guitars. (A blonde Strat, not that it matters).

Statement: I love to play. I love to listen. It is more than notes; more than technique; it is emotion. What I love best is sharing with others. There is no greater joy for me than giving; giving a smile, giving insight, giving help, providing aid to an emotion that would not have otherwise been felt. Music can be joy or sadness but it is a gift to be shared.

This one is very personal for me. Well, I guess all of the pages are. I have been playing and writing music since I was about 14; earlier if you count junior high band and the elementary school flutophone. The picture is of one of my Stratocasters that saw a lot of "road time". That being said, being a musician is not the point. It has been said that music is the universal language and that is an enabling concept of sentiment in the statement. Music carries emotion; it can calm, be uplifting, facilitate meditation, and very powerfully stir memories.

Music can be used intentionally for its calming or energizing impacts and is unconsciously part of our memories that happen in the process of living our lives. *Sharing* music is the biggest part of this topic. It really doesn't matter if you are a musician or if it is your music; sharing emotions and methods to evoke emotions can help others greatly. It is one of the gifts that is perpetual.

Another Day

> **Photo:** A unique opening in the clouds at sunrise over a hill with the silhouette of a tree in the opening.

> **Statement:** I have lived another day. I can see the sunrise and what a wonder it is that the days will pass and yet another will come. Today is a new day, a day of hope, a day to live the life that I have. What will I do today? How will I make it the best it can be?

It is probably obvious that this is about appreciating the simple things, appreciating the things that you do have, and living for today. The statement of "the best it can be", is intended to convey the concepts that context matters and everything is relative. The message is about accepting what you have, appreciating it, and working within that context, rather than wondering why you don't have more or why others didn't have something happen to them that happened to you. Move forward and experience the wonder of the day.

Fundamentals of Life

Don't Rain on My Parade

Photo: Sitting under an umbrella waiting for the parade in the rain with many others doing the same thing.

Statement: Where are you in this picture? Holding the umbrella? Walking in the rain? Feeling blue and waiting for it to be over or just holding your own? Outside influences over which we have no control are very disconcerting for many people. A little rain on your parade, literally, is probably not the most significant impact to many but what if you are the parade organizer and your career is based on the success of this one event? What if it is your last event as a senior in marching band? What if it is your one and only chance to see that one show before they retire? Regardless of how small or big this random occurrence is that interfered with your plans, it is a reality of life. In a recent adventure in cruising the back roads of rural Minnesota, I came upon a small shop with a small sign with small words that had big meaning. I bought two; one for me and one for my oldest daughter. It said, "Life is all about how you handle plan B"

I don't recall why I only bought two. Maybe it was all they had. I should have bought them for everyone in my family and everyone I know. I know they didn't have that many and I couldn't have afforded it anyway. The best I can do now is repeat the message. I have no idea who to give credit for this statement, but I wish I knew because it carries so much meaning in so few words. So many times in life the initial ideal plan does not work out. It is always good to be prepared or be willing and able to think fast rather than despair over the interruption to plan A. It is also not unusual for plan B to end up being better than plan A and probably more memorable. Plan A failing or needing adjustment is usually about plans that were outcome-based and something out of your control changed the path. Time for plan B, or C, or D, or…

Collaboration

Photo: My hand on the keys of a piano.

Statement: Do you see black and white or do you see a piano? There are obvious differences in appearance but the functions are the same and one without the other can create something simple but the breadth of music is extremely limited without both. Explore the differences, understand the commonality and embrace both.

This message is very similar to the previous *Look for the Constants*. The commonality matters far more than the differences. I am still trying hard to stay out of comments that are specific to society today, but I occasionally fail and this will be one of those times. The implication here is quite obvious without being stated; it is related to black and white as in a racial statement. It is such a sad thing to see the state of divide today. I grew up in the 60s and 70s and saw the cry for equality and being color-blind. I was in full support of what I understood the desire, ask, and demand to be. Judge people by their character, not by the color of their skin; admirable, logical, and ethical ask. That cry and demand has changed today and it is sad. Progress was made, although not complete, but that logical demand has turned into divisive rhetoric that demands a forcible look at and consideration of color. The ask is no longer to eliminate the consideration of color, but rather to treat people by the color of their skin rather than their character, talents, and principles. That demand is having such a negative impact on the previously desired outcome.

The literal analogy of the piano is very appropriate. The black keys are different in a number of ways other than color. They are different size, shape and name (sharps and flats). It is clear that a piano is not a piano without both. You can play a limited number of songs with all black or all white keys, but the universe of music is open with both. Limiting the use of either based on any of their superficial attributes only serves to limit and erode the concept and power of music.

Clearly, as stated in the chapter on equality, this concept does not only apply to black and white, it applies to anything superficial.

Lost in the Crowd

Photo: Underneath "the Bean" in Chicago.

Statement: It is easy to become lost in the crowd, or at least feel as though you are. When everything runs together and you cannot find yourself, you may question your significance if you cannot even see yourself in the mirror. Please understand that even when you step out of view of your own reflection, you are "in the picture" for someone else and if you can see them, they can see you. You do exist for them and your existence has a substance to their view of life. You make a difference even when you cannot see it.

The Bean is in a park in Chicago and it is really quite interesting to walk around and under it to see the distortions that are created.

It is sometimes easy to get lost in the crowd and feel like an anonymous, insignificant speck. If you look at a point in time, like the picture, it may be difficult to find yourself. Hold on to your grounding and rely on yourself. A view can be distorted from the outside, but only on the inside if you allow it. If you recognize yourself from the inside (your fundamentals), the outward impact is inevitable. You may never see the impact but the most simplistic action or event, planned or otherwise, will have an impact on others.

Look for the Light

Photo: The whole picture is very dark except for a few shadows that can indicate some forms of landscape and a small patch of bright sky breaking through the dark clouds.

Statement: Look for the light.

When all is dark, there is light to be found. The photo is obviously a literal view of that statement. The light might actually be literal but in many cases it is an analogy for hope. All is not dark unless you lose hope. In the case of the photo, if I had taken the photo an hour earlier, there would have been no visible light to the camera. Just as time passed and the sun rose, darkness will pass.

I will give you another literal example. The darkest place that I have been is in a cave. I took a tour and when we got to the lowest part that we were going, they turned off all lights. I had never experienced total darkness before and actually had no idea what total darkness even meant. You could put your own hand an inch from your face and have no idea that it was there. I could see that type of darkness leading to despair or fear, but a couple of things prevented that for me. I knew that this was a controlled situation and I had faith in the tour guide that they would turn the lights back on. I also had another light that was not so literal. There were people around me; there was a connection and there was even a sense of adventure.

This experiment touched on faith, hope, trust, perception, and so many of the topics because it forced me to look for a non-material connection to others and myself. If you have found an inner peace, you carry a light with you. It also made me realize that the times I thought I was in darkness before, I really was not.

Growth and Change

Photo: A hermit crab in a shell.
Statement: Allow yourself to grow and be open to change.

A hermit crab will grow and as it does, it will change shells to accommodate the growth. In not such a literal aspect, people will hopefully continue to grow and growth can change perspective and needs. If you are resistant to change, growth will be hampered and will stifle your potential, knowledge, wisdom, and the building of your inner core.

Don't be Afraid to Ruffle a Few Feathers – Blend in and Listen

Photo: The ruffled feathers photo is actually of a bird with ruffled feathers and the blend in photo is of a chameleon blending into the background.

Statement: Ruffled feathers statement is: Everyone will not always, if ever, agree. By standing up for what you believe, you may ruffle some feathers. In sharing your thoughts, you provide opportunity for others to learn and for you to respect yourself. Those who do not appreciate that are existing in their one-perception world, where everything is known and nothing is learned. The state of political correctness in this age has been a hindrance to social growth, freedom of expression, and a world where people can learn from each other. The chameleon statement is: Sometimes it's better to just blend in and listen.

Both of these photos are very much a literal representation of the statements and these concepts would seem to be contradictory. This is why I am addressing them together; the key is balance. The wording on these indicates that they are conceptual and contextual approaches. When you need answers or you see things going in a way that would impact your core principles, you should not be afraid to ruffle a few feathers. Living a life that is only based on making other people calm and happy will likely result in regrets, sadness, worry, disappointment, and other uncontrolled impacts. On the other hand, being a bully and not respecting the views, concerns, and principles of others is also not honorable, so sit back and listen. The context and timing clearly matters. A shorter way of putting this might be to not be a bully, but don't let yourself be bullied. That statement is a bit superficial but the point is that the two statements are not conflicting if you apply the context.

Another way, rather than deciding when to do one or the other, is to do both. Listening is most always a good idea and when you listen you have an opportunity to learn. After you have listened, your fundamentals and principles should guide your direction on the decision to share your position. It may be idealistic because it does not apply to all circumstances, but it is rare that someone's feathers being ruffled should get in the way of you applying your fundamentals and principles. Their feathers should not be your guide.

Let's look at a potential exception. Say that the situation where feathers might be ruffled is at work with your boss. Do you care more about your fundamentals or your boss's perception of you? The decision will likely include things like your financial situation, your career plans, and the mood of the boss on that given day. I can say that it is unfortunate if those are factors, but understandable why it is for some. How far do you *bend* your fundamentals, principles, and self-respect in that situation and how good do you feel about it? All sorts of factors drive these decisions, but once you have an opportunity to more deeply understand your fundamentals and who you are, it does get easier. One consideration that should take place is reassessment and tuning of your fundamentals. These situations that might cause you to feel justified in breaking your fundamentals might mean that your fundamentals and/or principles need tuning. I know that I said this earlier but I was once told that I was too principled to "make it" at work. It did hold me back from promotions and I was perfectly fine with being recognized for being principled. I did not try to *unnecessarily* ruffle feathers, but I would not lie for or lie to corporate management or break my fundamentals and principles in order to gain favor.

Relative Perspective – Everything is Relative

Photo: The appearance of large rocks on a hill with a very faded soldier climbing up a lower part of the hill.

Statement: This is probably my biggest, most pervasive and yet simplistic observation (everything is simple…); it applies to everything! I could present the picture to the left with little context and let you draw your own perspective. I can add the context represented by the false image on this page or I can tell you that these massive rocks sit on a nightstand and the largest is less than 3" across. Each additional piece of information can change the context but has not changed the facts. Our language, our communication, or lack thereof, and our thoughts are based on the relative nature of our perceptions. Our perceptions are our truth. There is nothing deliberate about the nature of relativity; it hides behind the scenes and confuses the ability to relate to one another. When you say big, there is the potential for a complete disconnect in my meaning and yours. My big may be your little, my soft your hard, my rich your poor, my beauty your ugly, etc. If your perception is your truth and

Part 3: Coffee Table

> mine is my truth then …? If there are two versions of the truth, which one is real or is neither? How do we communicate? How do we find the facts?

This topic overlapped the topics of truth, fact, and perception. That was inevitable since relativity is a perception and once you talk about perception the question of fact comes into play.

How do we ever communicate? We make assumptions and move on, in many cases thinking that we are in alignment when we are not. Those people that have similar training, education, and experiences are more likely to be aligned. If dentists talk to each other, or network engineers talk to each other about their trade, it is more likely that they will use terms that will have a common definition. It does not mean they will agree, but they are more likely to understand. In the case of more generic topics and language, it is far less likely. If I say that I am going to send you a check soon, I may be of the mindset that soon may be within a month and you may think soon is in the next 5 minutes. Much of this has been discussed in other areas of the book such as the discussions of communication and listening.

Another aspect that we talked about is the misuse and intentional misrepresentation that can happen with words, the lack of words, and even images. I saw it with my own eyes! Take this photo; it was an intentional misdirection to emphasize the nature of relativity. Starting off, the image of the rocks was taken from an angle to intentionally create a perspective of size bigger than fact. The soft representation of a soldier climbing the hill on which the rocks sit is actually a small toy army man and the haziness of soft touch of this part of the picture is to help hide the fact of it being a toy army man and also to make it a subtle reference to size that may not even be noticed but sensed in determining the perspective. You saw it with your own eyes, but you probably saw what someone wanted you to see. I am not suggesting that everything you see is being manipulated, but you should always be aware that it is possible.

Truth – It's a Fact???

Photo: This is just the word TRUTH.

Statement: Does "real truth" really exist? I believe that there are a few circumstances that qualify as "real" truth beyond that which is derived from your perception or your faith. They are very few and once you cross that line you enter the realm of opinion in which all you can best hope for is an increased probability of being correct. The real facts lie past and present and then only in the what, not the why. A new official record high was set for Madeup City, MN. The what is that it is the new highest on record. Is it the highest ever? We don't know. The cause of this (the why) is an opinion with debatable degrees of probability. The other category of fact is mathematical derivatives. These must be derived from either real facts or from conditional arguments. Presuming we are all in the same language and numeric base system, then 2+2=4 is an agreed to fact. If a=b and b=c, then a=c is a fact without knowing the fact of what a, b or c equals. A being equal to c, however, is dependent on that big IF that opens the statement. Of all the words spoken and written, there is very little that is truly fact. They are presented as facts but we are living on probabilities most of the time. Accepting this decreases the likelihood of arrogance and increases the probability of humility. The more I understand – the less I know. So how do we live without truth? Can truth be derived from the most common beliefs? If most believe it, it must be true. Not likely; consider the world being flat for example. They were wrong but they were all in agreement. The "smart" people will decide? Whose truth gets to decide who the smart people are? Let science decide? It was science that determined the earth was flat. Science evolves, the real truth does not. Let God decide? This may work for those that may know what God knows. Waiting for God to decide or defining how God decides may lead to religious wars. So we live with facts of the past, our perception, faith, hope and varying degrees of probability.

That was a mouthful! What more could there be to say? This topic was pervasive in this book so I will just make two general statements.

First, be leery of those stating facts, especially if it relates to something that is *going to* happen or why something did happen. There is much of that going on today in this world as I suspect there has always been. Regardless of the title that a person holds or the education they have, be leery.

Second, just because something is not fact does mean that it should be disregarded. There is potentially very useful information in the misstatement of fact that can provide perceptions and probabilities for consideration in your own conclusions.

Distorted View

Photo: A wide angle round mirror reflecting riders on a merry-go-round.

Statement: Sometimes our view becomes distorted. This may surface as depression, narrow-mindedness, reclusion, crabbiness, stupidity, or many other labels that can be put on another person. Focus can be a very good thing as long as it doesn't close out everything else and distort your point of view to a warped, myopic, black and white world. Be conscious of all and enjoy the ride.

This may seem the same as *Lost in the Crowd* at first look. While the concept of the pictures is the same, in that they are a distorted reflection, the message is different. This, in itself, is a good message of how people can see, understand, and learn different things from the same experience.

The caution in this message is to not let focus become consuming to the point where the outside world has no impact. This is not the same as being focused on your self-things. This type of focus does not have to be on self, but it is singular and lets no other inputs in. It tends to distort reality, where your narrow focus *is* your world and everything is black and white.

Freedom

Photo: The liberty bell and a homeless person.

Statement: The freedom to express, freedom to worship, freedom to be alone, freedom to… What does it mean to you? Do we search for "controlled" freedom in order to avoid anarchy? Are freedom and laws contradictory? Is there such a thing as controlled freedom? Where do we draw the line? Is the line when you hurt someone else? What is hurt? You hurt my feelings, you hurt my eyes, and those plaid pants make me sick. Can the homeless person sleep in public? Is that freedom? We all seek to control our own space. When does our space touch another and where does freedom go when it does?

Freedom is one of those things that I believe is greatly underappreciated. It concerns me that the people that have freedom have lost sight of its value or even what it means. Real freedom includes the freedom to fail.

Part 3: Coffee Table

I asked questions in the statement related to this photo regarding where the line is. Is the line when you hurt someone else? And then, what is hurt? We can talk about the theoretical line and the practical line. The utopian theoretical line could be defined by not hurting others and everybody would have the same understanding of hurt and everybody would be respectful of others. We can want that, but that is not the reality of this world. There is not a universal understanding of *hurt*. Many people are not respectful. Does that mean that you should not be? Of course not. It also does not mean that you give up your freedom and your beliefs because someone else is not respectful. This is where the hard decisions arise again; this is similar to the *Ruffling Feathers* discussion. This type of lack of respect conflicting with other's freedoms and beliefs are the makings of war.

Before delving into the theory of war, let's look at the practical intersection of freedoms that hurt others. I did not ask the question about the definition of hurt only for the obvious examples that I gave. Should someone not be able to wear plaid pants because it makes someone else "sick"? People can wear what they want and people that don't like it don't have to look. This gets into the discussion of whether the hurt can be avoided. If by turning your head or closing your eyes you can avoid the hurt, it is probably not real hurt but someone that just needs to get a grip and be a little more tolerant and respectful. "But I don't want to turn my head!" Tough! If everybody got everything they wanted in every way, nobody would have anything and the world would end. I am realizing how far I am already going down this very deep hole. But, I am going to go a little bit further because freedom does encompass at least three of the fundamentals; love, believing, and honor. And if freedom fades too far from reality, hope comes into play.

Back to the practicality and hope for common sense. Common sense has become close to an oxymoron because common sense seems to no longer be common. I asked another question about controlled freedom. People do like to control others when it comes to making themselves more comfortable. What if I want the freedom to do something against the law? That is truly an oxymoron. If there are laws, laws are to be respected and nobody is given the "freedom" to break the laws. Of course there are always extenuating circumstances but, as a practice, it does not exist. There is a line that, for most circumstances, is well-defined. There generally are not laws against hurting someone's feelings although we could be moving in that dangerous direction.

Where is freedom legitimately curtailed and do laws curtail freedom or do laws enable freedom? People can enter into a contract with terms that limit freedom under the terms of the contract. This only limits the freedoms in the direct context of the contract. The one that is most familiar is an employment contract. Many might say that they do not have a contract but they do. When an employer hires an employee, it would be very strange for there not to be terms of the employment. You could consider the terms of employment as being laws for this purpose, but the difference is that you can walk away from your employment. It is certainly more difficult to walk away from governmental laws unless you leave the city, state, or country in which they are in effect. As an example, an employer can mandate how you dress at work or when representing the company. They can require that you work certain hours and in certain locations. They can require pretty much anything that is not against the law because your agreement with them for employment is voluntary and if you don't like the terms, you still have freedom; quit or don't take the job in the first place. Another example at work can impact freedom of speech. The same principles apply to that. You have the option to leave.

My understanding of human nature and the realities of our world make it difficult for me to believe that freedom is possible without laws. With that belief, freedom is freedom within the law. When you include freedom to challenge the law, this seems like the best that could be reasonably be expected. Even with laws, people still try to remove freedoms from others. This usually looks like a person not liking what someone else does, thinks, or says. Freedom and respect have a dependent relationship.

Nothing is Simple, and… Everything is Simple

Photo: A couple of hand written formulas; one simple and one complex.

Statement: How can it be both? Primarily by perception. It is very important to recognize both the simple and complex in order to keep a balance. The fact is that things are what they are regardless of how you see them or assess or distress over them. In philosophy, logic is represented by formulas (mind your Ps and Q$\underline{s}$). I find it very beneficial, in fact imperative, to find the simplicity in the situation. What are the things that are irrelevant to the situation? What things cancel out? What is the root cause? What are the common denominators? The lowest common denominator is at the core of the most simplistic resolution to a complex formula or situation. Arriving at the lowest common denominator can be achieved by complex assessment, previous experience, pure luck or a number of other ways. Hoping for luck is acceptable, counting on it is foolish. I once saw a poster that was both funny and accurate. It showed a room with a number of lab coat donned geeks standing around a large mainframe computer trying to figure out why it wasn't working. The view of the computer showed the power cord laying on the floor just short of the outlet. The caption read "Look for the simple first". What are the things that are essential to your problem, to your life, to your solution? These are not usually the things that are first thought of in a problematic situation but are very often the solution. The things that are most important and at the "core" are the things that will impact and resolve the most. Whether you reach the conclusion through complex assessment, prior experience, prioritization of your values or pure luck, the solution is often simple. The closer you get to simple, the more effective the solution. The term oversimplification comes from finding a simple perspective with no appreciation of the underlying complexity or the fact that simple does not necessarily mean easy. Respect the complexity and discover the simple. The complex formula contains a section that is complex and contains variables that might not be resolved but it is ultimately multiplied by zero, making it irrelevant to the solution. Don't get buried in the details before considering the importance of the bigger picture. Understand the rules and the context. What might change the answer to 2+2?

While this is a very long statement, the intention of this is to provoke thought and not make assumptions. Clearly, some things are complicated and some things are simple under certain circumstances. The circumstances or context, as has been discussed so many times, can make a significant amount of difference to understanding, perceptions, and solutions. Contributing to the ability to simplify the complex and understand the complexity of the simple are your previous experiences and the lessons or patterns learned from those experiences. The mathematical formulas are a "simple" way of expressing a very complex topic. If you understand that anything multiplied by zero is zero, it makes anything that is multiplied by zero irrelevant. If a number or variable minus itself is zero, then it doesn't matter what the number is. If a very complex computer system is not working, there is no need to understand the complexity of the inner workings of the computer if it is not plugged in.

This is more than just looking for the simple answer, it is applying previous learnings and the patterns that you have created in your knowledge base to new situations as well as applying your fundamentals and priorities to eliminate the irrelevant.

I'll give you one quick example. Let's say you do a lot of online shopping for clothes and you have noticed that sometimes the clothes are poor quality and they are sometimes very small. Upon further assessment you determine that all of the poor quality and small sizes are from a particular country. Of the many millions of options available online, eliminating clothes from this country eliminates the noise of more than a million of the options. This is an example that is not significant to important aspects of your life, but patterns can apply to anything.

Walk the Path

Photo: A secluded path along a winding river.

Statement: Walk a path of direction and determination but flow with the curves that life will provide.

This is probably well summed by with the comments earlier about "plan B". Just because there are bends in the road, it does not have to prevent forward progress.

Fear

Photo: A dark photo of a cat peering through a leaded glass window.

Statement: Next to love, it is probably the most disabling emotion. What do you fear? What do you fear most? Most fears are about things that are not real in that they are not happening and are unlikely to happen. So why is there so much fear? What image represents fear for you? There are certainly things that are scary but that is different than fear. My use of the word fear is based on fear as a state of mind as opposed to being afraid in a situation of immediate danger. That type of danger raises the fight or flight response and can help to protect you. That fight or flight response can also be triggered by fear and that becomes disabling rather than preserving. I am not talking about caution. Caution is a healthy consideration of potential risk. The bottom line is that Roosevelt's statement rings very true; "All we have to fear is fear itself" [51]. The most disabling fear is of fear. To those who face this fear, I first hope that you are able to see what it is that you really fear, because most see it as imminent danger rather than fear (I have been there). Once you find the real fear, only then are you able to find your way free. The shedding of fear, regardless of how small, is very freeing.

Fear, combined with worry was a long chapter in Part 2 and I answered some of these questions for me personally. It is still up to you to answer for yourself, but the concept and patterns are the same. They are not only the same, they are common.

The photo maybe looks a little eerie to those that do not know the facts of the photo. The photo is actually of my former cat sitting on a railing outside my front door window. He was a very calm and gentle cat. Information can dramatically change the perspective of fear and your reaction.

Peace

Photo: A very faded washed-out photo of a sunset over water.

Statement: Peace exists in the absence of fear.

I talked a lot about inner peace in this book. It is actually a desired outcome of the whole concept of fundamentals. This page is not specific to inner peace but it is certainly related. My belief is that you can have inner peace and still occasionally be impacted by fear. It is possible to be at peace with yourself, including the reality of fears that may be part of your life, as long as they are not breaking your fundamentals or principles or controlling your life.

The peace referred to in this page of the Coffee Table book is about the type of peace that is an engulfing *calm*. That peace is not likely to be a perpetual state for anyone and cannot exist *at the same moment* as fear.

Battle Between Good and Evil

Photo: The head and shoulders of a golden statue of a woman that fades to the next page in a swirling spiral.

Statement: We may be losing the battle. Do you believe that people are generally good? Some still believe that but I am not one of them. Of course, that depends on your definition and perspective of what is good. I believe that we are on a downward spiral and that spiral is spinning so fast that we have lost the relative perspective to what used to be called good. I don't think that everyone is in that spiral but it is getting harder and harder to find those that aren't. The culture as a whole is definitely spinning. People rationalize their goodness in relative perspective to the lack of goodness that exists in the spiral. Greed, selfishness and the expectation of something for nothing abound. This makes it even more important that you measure yourself against your values rather than others. That is the only way to keep the spiral from consuming us all. This may sound fatalistic, but I do have hope and faith and a strong belief in good. What do you believe?

This was written ten years ago and my opinion has not changed.

The vast majority of the Coffee Table book has a very positive attitude and encouraging tone, so why this topic and the next (Evil)? These two topics, and maybe one other, have caused the perception of the book to change for some, to the point that one person has called the book "dark". This gives me reason to spend a little more time on these topics. It's fine that people have their own opinion, but in this case I want to try to further explain, not defend, my intent.

When I make statements about not being a person that believes that people are generally good and that the world around us is in a downward spiral, it is understandable that some might think that I have a very negative, if not fatalistic, view. I do believe in good and I do believe that there is hope for most people, but the broad statement of *people in general* being generally good is not what my experience tells me. People will form their perspective based on their perception and their environment and it becomes relative to their surrounding unless they have found their fundamentals and their grounding points. I don't know about you, but I am not willing to bet that everybody in the world has found their fundamentals and is living by them. Many people are followers and like to fit in, and as the herd moves so do the rest.

Following does not make you bad or evil, nor does it make you good. It relinquishes you, your power, and your direction to someone else. Therefore, if what someone else does is not in the best interest of you or others, you contribute to that by following. The more we lose sight of some grounding point, the easier it is for that to happen. When you combine the concept of following with the possibility that those who are leading have motives that are driven by greed or their own self-interest at the expense of others, the volume of people driving toward "good" becomes less.

Look at the way that things have changed in your lifetime, regardless of your age but of course the older you are the more change you will have seen. When you identify a change, ask yourself *why* you think that change happened. What drove that change and what is the impact of that change? Whose life did it make better and at what cost? Things that used to not be okay are now okay - why is that? Who and how did it help?

If you simply look at the different philosophies outlined toward the beginning of this book, you will see that some philosophies are not what some people might consider "nice" or healthy for society. There is such a wide variety. Then look at crime and the way many people treat other people in general and to me it is evident that all people are not displaying "good" behavior. Are they inherently good? If they are, why are they not acting that way? Greed is real, crime is real, hate is real, and evil is real. This does not mean that I believe that *most* people are not capable of being good. I believe it is possible for most; however, with the influences around people and the lack of grounding, I do believe the probability is very high that it will not exist for most. It will for some.

This is obviously my perspective and you may or may not subscribe to it. I honestly wish that I didn't believe it. My purpose in writing all of this is not to be judgmental or tell you that you or others are bad or evil. My purpose is to share the thought that there can be a fair amount of people that do not have your best interest in mind and you will benefit from not only being cautious, but also grounding yourself in your fundamentals. The more people *allow* it to happen, the harder it is to see.

Evil

Photo: The head of a horned bull type mask with fire showing in its mouth and in the background.

Statement: Unfortunately, the evil that we encounter is rarely as obvious as this representation. If it were, we could easily choose to avoid it if we so desired. In fact, we would likely run away. Some associate evil with something to fear and look for scary things. Evil is not something to fear but rather something to acknowledge. The knowledge and recognition of evil gives us the opportunity and power to control our interaction with it. This does not have to take on religious connotations unless you want it to. There is good in this world and there is evil. There are many actions that are neither and many things that are neither. The judgment of everything, every action, and everyone that you encounter is not only unnecessary, but pious. Keep your eyes open to where evil may lie and your heart open to good. Know your right and wrong and trust yourself once you do.

It was not intentional, nor did I even realize it until I started writing this, that the photos taken for these two themes of *The Battle Between Good and Evil* and *Evil*, were taken in Las Vegas. There is no intentional or inferred correlation between the topics and the location of the photos.

Evil does not wear a mask or look scary in a way that makes you want to run away. It is inviting and tempting and makes you feel like you belong. It can take all of your fabric to identify it. This is the power of evil and it can be very hard not to follow. I also want to follow up on the point that the lack of good is not necessarily evil. Mistakes can be made by people with bad outcomes and that does not make it evil. Evil has an intent that consumes its followers. Again, I can see where someone would say this is "dark". The world is a real place and it makes sense that you are aware of all of the realities and keep your eyes, heart, mind, and soul sharp and prepared to defend your inner core. This should not be a scary and dark discussion but an empowerment for you. You can be stronger than evil, but not without recognizing it.

Thou Shalt not Steal - Respect

Photo: Photo 1: A beat-up and rusty pop machine chained to a building. Photo 2: The respect photo is very faded but there are various people on the street, some reading a paper, playing guitar, drinking, hugging, and carrying on with their lives.

Statement: Statement 1: Thou shalt not steal. Statement 2: Respect others! Always! Treat people with respect; all people. Respect what is others. Treat the things that are not yours with as much care as you would treat your most treasured possessions. To others it may be that and it is not yours to judge if you are in a position of using something of someone else's. Do not abuse the generosity of others. Is it respectful to be politically correct? Is the correct term today African-American? Really? Does respect change from day to day? Are white people from Africa that are naturalized to the US, not African-American? What is the purpose, the heritage or the color of the skin? Certainly there are people with dark skin that are not from Africa. This is not a topic about race or religion or any other political agenda that breeds separation…that is the point. It is respect for the unique individuals that we are and the values that respect everyone. Respect should not break your core values, it may however, fly in the face of your truth since your truth is your perception. Classifications in the name of PC generally promote division of underlying commonalities and create positions of deception. I could state that I am a gray-haired, slightly past middle age, Norwegian American and still not define who I am. Those labels do not define us; we are people and stating all of the facts of our external characteristics arguably prevents people from seeing who we are, discovering commonalities and sharing knowledge, values and perceptions.

I obviously combined two photos in this segment. I did this because they are so closely related. Certainly, if you respect laws or people, you would not steal. So why make a point of the stealing aspect related to the lack of respect? The photo of the pop machine chained to the building *implies* that there has been a problem with people stealing the pop machine. This is a very beat-up and rusted machine and it sits on the porch of a very small store, in a very, very small town with very little around. Maybe that photo conjures up other thoughts for you, but with the assumption that theft has been a problem it leads to *why*. Someone would steal the machine for the pop, for the change, or for the thrill? It is not necessary to steal the machine to get the pop or the change. The further story on this that relates to respect is why someone would go to so much effort to chain a very dilapidated machine to a building. It would seem as though to them it was a valuable possession. How could that be? Who are we to say what is of value to others? That is not a judgment that we should make. A quite elderly lady who lived in the back of the store with her handicapped daughter ran this store. They had no register and just had a piece of paper, a calculator and a box for money when you checked out in the store.

This statement also touched on race and skin color. This is another common theme related to not judging a book by its cover and taking the time to look below the surface and a number of other topics. People can be so judgmental and controlling that divisiveness is almost inevitable. What is a surprise is the source of many of the instigations of division. How can it be that the people that want respect demand that the method of gaining respect is to disrespect others and to call out the mechanism that supported the division initially as the method that will be used to remove it? Somewhere along the line the message becomes incomprehensible and far from respectful.

This can easily slide from respect to the phrase of being *fair* that we discussed in the chapter on equality. Respect must be color-blind. Fairness must be color-blind. Equal opportunity must be color-blind. All of these things must be color-blind in all regard and the way to solve for them, for some, is to force the consideration of color. Respect of qualities and of the real person cannot consider color. I have been emphasizing color because it comes up a lot but the same is true for any superficial characteristics; tall, short, skinny, fat, young, old, and all other characteristics that are irrelevant to the person that exists within.

Old

Photo: Two "old" ladies on motorcycles.

Statement: OLD is most certainly a state of mind that can often be postponed.

These "old ladies" were actually sitting on these motorcycles. They both had a love of life and adventure. They happened to be mother and daughter and they were both in their eighties at the time of the pictures. The photos were taken about 30 years apart. This is the only picture in the book that I did not take other than the picture of myself. These photos came from family archives and I put them together. It was not to deceive that I put them together. It was as a gift to the daughter in the picture and she had it hanging on her wall in the nursing home. Everything is not as it seems and the "elderly" should not be discounted. This is also one of those subjects related to looking below the surface and not judging a book by its cover.

Some say that you are only old if you feel old. Age will certainly have a physical impact that will eventually change what you can do or the way that you can do it, but it does not have to end everything. I personally feel much younger in mind and spirit than my body allows for me to do or the mirror tells me is so. Age is sneaky! It tells others that you are old and changes their perception of you, but you are left out of that communication. You go on as you would until you are told by your body or by others that you are no longer who you think you are. Wait, but you feel like you're the same person. You are. In fact you may be better.

It is often that physical age and mental age get out of sync. When you are young, you may feel that you are older than you are and are "entitled" to do older things and be respected like you were older. When you are older, you may feel like you are younger and feel that you should be able to do younger things and be respected as though you were younger.

This page is labeled as *Old*, but it well could be labeled as "Age". It is not that age is irrelevant, it is that age is often confused with who the person is.

Beam Me Up

Photo: Two girls standing in the woods with their arms raised and their bodies are partly faded.

Part 3: Coffee Table

Statement: Sometimes we just want to say "Beam me up Scotti". But we all know Scotti is not going to do it.

Sometimes we just want to get out of this place because it can get so crazy. Some will take a healthy momentary break with relaxation. Some will take a vacation. Some will withdraw to a much darker place. Scotti is not going to zap you away, so it is up to you to find your escape. The escape that I refer to is not running away, it is taking a break and we all need breaks at some point. It is a healthy mechanism to maintain your perspective and reground. It would be unhealthy to ignore the need for the break and let it break you.

I speak of *it* breaking you. What is *it* to you? When you know, you can address it. For many it is stress and the next obvious question would be what is causing the stress? We discussed many possibilities as well as ways to address them in Part 2 of this book. Think about the things in your inner core.

Look Below the Surface

Photo: Red rock dwelling area walls. As you look at the wall, two carved out holes could be eyes and looking closer shows further face shape.

Statement: Take the time to look below the surface.

This is similar to *Old* and a number of the other topics. If you take the time to look and not judge by what you initially see, your eyes will open to whole new worlds and ways of thinking. Your knowledge will grow and your respect for the simple and the depth of complexity will flourish.

Once in a While

Photo: A Photoshopped image of a person peeking out from behind a very skinny tree that they would obviously not fit behind.

Statement: Once in a while peek out from your world and see what is happening in the worlds around you. It is easy to get absorbed in your own space and lose track of all the things around us. This also has the parallel effect of the "outer worlds" not even knowing you are there. Observe and make yourself known.

Outer worlds? Arguably, we all live in our own world with our own experiences, our own perceptions, and our own truths, which results in our own version of reality. Our reality is our world. When we get so absorbed in our perceptions, there can be little room for alternatives and the opportunity for learning and growth. Staying in our own world also removes the interactions with others, the sharing of ideas, and opportunity for others to grow.

An important balance is staying true to you (the positive and internal) but being open to listening, learning, and seeing the worlds around you.

Show and tell

Photo: "I love Samantha and Kelsey" painted in a very sloppy and big manner on an interior house wall.

Statement: Don't waste an opportunity to play show and tell with your love.

I was painting my living room and was not going to be able to finish that day. It was a great opportunity to use that chore to leave a message for my children and painted "I love Samantha and Kelsey" on the wall before painting it over the next day. This is really about one of the core fundamentals (love) and having it top of mind to think of others and the willingness, if not the need, to let them know that you love them. Love felt and internalized can have value but it blooms when you share it. Tell someone.

Merry Christmas

Photo: A cat wearing a Santa hat.

Statement: As I write this, it is Christmas Eve and the thought of it not being acceptable to greet someone with a Merry Christmas is, at a minimum, annoying to me. I grew up with Christmas, as did most people in the US; it is part of who I am. It is part of this country; it is a national holiday, at least for now. Whether you celebrate Christmas as a religious event or not, the day is widely recognized and celebrated. Forcing the greeting to a generic "happy holidays" seems to imply that there is something wrong with the word Christmas or with something related to it. Is it offensive to call the Fourth of July Independence Day or any of the other national holidays by its name? Why Christmas? Have we gone WAY too far in political correctness? Have the controlling wishes of a few become far more important than being real and respectful? I would suggest that others be able to live their life within their cultural traditions and I would not expect that I need to change my traditions and culture to accommodate those that are far less tolerant than I. Give me common sense and respect any day, so... MERRY CHRISTMAS.

When I initially wrote this, I was expecting rejection or negative reactions to this topic but I have not received that feedback. It may be that I just have not heard it. I thought that people might interpret my words as being intolerant of others, their culture and their religion. Maybe I did a good job of explaining that, but my experience has been that saying Merry Christmas has been seen by a very intolerant group of people as a very bad thing. It is not that I expect everybody to say Merry Christmas; it is that I believe that I should be able to say it, just as others should be able to express their greetings related to their culture/beliefs. To not allow that is quite intolerant of others. I do believe in respecting others and being honorable, and it is not a bad thing to expect the same from others.

It is probably evident that this topic is not just about Christmas, but Christmas is a good representation of just how far some will go and have gone. Why would someone be offended by the words Merry Christmas? It is evident to me that intolerance is a major part of it but it goes beyond that; it is about control. Why would anybody even have the slightest desire to control a cultural or religious greeting of another person? This relates to so many other topics such as freedom. Does it *hurt* someone if someone else says Merry Christmas?

Beauty

Photo: Three pages with three *beauty* photos; one of Mount McKinley from the air, one of a butterfly, and one of flowers.

Statement: Beauty comes in majestic forms and in insect forms... But most often in more subtle forms. Things that you see or experience every day. Beauty is more available than we sometimes recognize. A smile, an act of kindness, dew on the grass, a cloud, a

> weed, a bird, a reflection, a building, a sound and an endless array of memory-worthy spontaneous beauty.

Beauty covers three pages and it could be far more. This section is probably suited well for being coupled with *Appreciation*. Appreciation is much broader than just appreciating beauty, but there are so many forms of beauty it is worth separating this section from *Appreciation*. It is also applicable to *Slow*. If you slow down, there is beauty to be found. It does not have be the type of beauty that slaps you in the face such as the photo of the mountain in the book. That is Mt. McKinley and it is truly majestic; it is hard not to recognize its beauty.

As I looked at describing the various photos on this topic and the intent of the message, I realized that all three photos are of nature. That is a message unto itself and was not my original thought. Beauty comes in so many forms. People can be beautiful; so too can paintings, sculptures, photographs, buildings, poetry, words, thoughts, souls, and the list goes on. There is so much beauty in the world that it can probably be found *anywhere*.

The things that prevent us from seeing beauty are usually within ourselves. Moving too fast to see them and being of a mindset that refuses to recognize them are two major reasons they evade us. If we are depressed, our focus is on despair and our ability to recognize beauty is compromised. Depression is an obvious example, but so many people ignore or fail to recognize the beauty that is all around. I am certainly not saying that everybody should walk around doing nothing but recognizing beauty and being the happy hippie flowerchild with flowers in their hair. There is a balance with all things. The point is that beauty is all around and when we need a break from the rat race, it is there for the taking and we should take it more often.

Fundamentals of Life

Comfort

Photo: A mother holding a small child close.

Statement: Somewhere between sadness and elation lies a very desirable place. It can include those ranges of emotions or none of those because it is safe. That feeling of safety; where you are home. You are loved and no one questions or criticizes. You can hold or be held; both have their own comfort and their own rewards.

People find comfort in various ways and in various objects and actions. Someone can bring comfort to someone else by their actions. People can find comfort in a blanket or in food. Comfort is a state of calm and warmth that can have an engulfing feeling of being safe. The length of time that feeling of comfort lasts has extreme variations. It can be a fleeting moment or something that lasts days. People will talk about a comfortable lifestyle, but within that it is likely that the feeling and emotion of comfort may not be persistent. People living a life that is commonly thought of as comfortable, will have their own trials and tribulations to address. This emphasizes again that everything is relative. You can look at the trials of a "comfortable" person compared to a person that struggles to live or have the most basic needs met and find comparable emotional desperation. You might say that one can surround themselves with comforts, but the comfort to which I refer is emotional. The physical comforts, do not buy comfort of the heart and soul. Money can't buy love, happiness, or this type of comfort.

Slow

Photo: The very end of a dock and overlooking a lake with a horizon that has the sun almost dark behind the trees.

Statement: Find a place to be slow; a place to contemplate and understand yourself separate from all of the things that are pushing and pulling on you. This does not have to be a physical place but it may help initially in the separation. When you are feeling out of control or when things are moving too fast, this place can allow you to be you and assess your values and priorities. Ideally, this is a state of mind that you are able to take with you wherever you go and call upon whenever it is needed.

Is this feeling repetitive yet? It probably was a long time ago. The message is similar to *Beauty, Comfort, Appreciation,* and a number of others, but they are expressed with different photos and with slightly different approaches. The idea of all of these variants is to bring real examples of the higher message.

Glow

Photo: A close-up of a flower that appears to be glowing from the inside.

Statement: Tap the inner-glow. There are things within you that have more strength than the darkness around you. Let them prevail.

People are generally stronger than they think they are. An inner glow can come from a place that includes confidence and a willingness to believe and trust in yourself. This could be the photograph of your inner core. Not only is there beauty all around, there is beauty and a glow from within that may be stronger than you think.

Strengths

Photo: There is a VERY faded photo on this page of a high school show choir overwritten by words that include Compassion, Math, Sports, Story Telling, Friend, Smiling, Integrity, Honesty, and the statement, "An endless set of strengths exist".

Statement: Everybody has strengths. While it is important to recognize that you have them and learn how to use them, it is just as important to recognize that others have them as well. It is very likely that theirs are different than yours. This would mean that if you share, you could both benefit. The only way to benefit is to respect others and the idea that everyone has something special to offer. It really is possible to learn from the seemingly unlikely candidate.

This use of respect does not include trust in the person, but rather that people have their own opinions, talents, strengths, and freedom. In one of my many careers, I was working with mentally handicapped children and creating behavior modification programs. That is a book unto itself. The reason that I bring it up here is there was a boy that had a very low IQ and did not speak. He had a behavior that involved swinging objects back and forth. A yoyo would be a perfect object to use. He was creative enough to meet his individual needs in that nothing would stop him from finding a way to swing something. One of the most creative was pulling a string from a piece of clothing slowly enough to get something about a foot long and "tying" it to a marble. You try that. I certainly learned that it was possible to do that, but it is not a skill that I think I probably will need. What I did have reinforced is that everybody has strengths and that perseverance can achieve unbelievable things. Both of those are good lessons from what might be an unexpected source.

Fly Like an Eagle Even if You're Not

> **Photo:** A seagull flying low over a beach with another seagull on the sand. The flying gull is casting a shadow.

> **Statement:** You can hang your head and feel inferior in the shadow but when you raise your head, you see that others much like you are doing great things and casting majestic shadows. Get out there.

The title would imply a photo of an eagle, which it is not. You do not have to be an eagle to cast the shadow of an eagle or have the impact of an eagle. You do not have to be a giant to cast a giant shadow. Impact is not proportional to your stature or physical attribution. If you looked only at the shadow cast by the seagull and could not see the seagull, you could make a very convincing argument that it was an eagle.

Impacting others and the whole world around you can come from anyone with any background. Casting the shadow of an eagle relies on your inner core where you find your self-things such as self-confidence. If you believe in you, your shadow will follow.

Learn From the Past

> **Photo:** Photos in an Army museum of historical figures.

> **Statement:** Learn from the past – yours and others but focus on the future.

Fundamentals of Life

The phrase, "history repeats itself" comes to mind. I am not sure how literal that phrase was meant to be or how literally it is taken, but I see it falling into the process of learning and acquiring knowledge. I am sure that many people think that things that happened historically or to others has no real bearing on them. Some things just do not change contrary to the statement from 500 BC about change. Consequences of actions and human nature may change but, in principle, very slowly.

The exact same circumstances are not likely to repeat but the patterns repeat over and over; cause and effect, again not from the precise literal perspective, but from the perspective of patterns. A simple physical example of one would be if you touch a hot stove, you will get burned. Translate that into a pattern of, if you touch anything hot, it will hurt. That history will repeat itself over and over and you should not have to experience it over and over to understand that. Ideally, you don't have to experience it at all if you learn from the history of others. Finding the patterns is often not as obvious as touching something hot. Go back to finding the "simple" part of the circumstance and that is likely a good place to start for finding a pattern.

This photo was taken at Ft. Benning Infantry Museum. This is not about war or the Army or anything like that, but a lot of thought process around history repeating itself comes from that genre. There are patterns, behaviors and cause and effect relationships, as well as general human nature that are useful for future events and decisions. This is a major contributor to wisdom. I have offered some of my history and knowledge acquired throughout this book with hopes that you will be able to benefit.

Leave a Mark

Photo: An Oceanside beach with a person in the distance and footprints in the foreground.

> **Statement:** You leave a mark wherever you go. What will your mark look like?

The footprints in the sand are leaving a mark where my wife has walked. Clearly, the photo is a physical representation of something more meaningful. Everyone leaves a mark on this world. I believe it is impossible not to. There are some that feel they are insignificant, but everyone impacts others and those people impact other people and the impacts are viral and most often not traceable.

For me, this is one of the primary considerations of my fundamentals and my priorities. The impact that a person has on the world is likely never known to that person, but every decision that you make has a potential impact on others even if that is not part of your intent.

On Golden

> **Photo:** A lake with fall colored trees and a house sitting on the shore across the lake.

> **Statement:** Regardless of your choices along the way and regardless of where you end up, find yourself, be true to yourself, love and appreciate everything that you have in your heart. No one can take that away. If only you could have found it and learned it earlier. If only you could share what you know now with those that have not yet figured it out. In the end, all we can do is try. We can give, but it may not be received. Regardless, share it all, live it all, love it all; for in the end, regrets are the hardest to accept.

For those that know the movie "On Golden Pond", the script of the movie adds more context to this statement. It might also add context to why this photo is associated with this statement. This photo was actually taken in the place where much of the scenery in that movie was filmed. I see this photo as being *the* Golden Pond.

This page in the Coffee Table book is as close as it can get to a short statement that summarizes why I continue to write. I am driven by purpose, intent, love, sharing, a genuine need to try to have a positive impact, and a hope that it will happen.

Peace be with You

> **Photo:** The final photo in the book is a sunset across the ocean where both the clouds and the water look a very subtle shade of purple.

> **Statement:** Tomorrow is a new day and each new day presents new opportunities and new challenges. Greet them with the peace of your mind and the strength of your heart.

Your peace of mind is your inner peace and the strength of your heart is the combination of your self-things. This is your inner core and your strength.

Part 3: Coffee Table

Set Sail

Photo: Another sunset across the ocean with a sailboat shadowed in the horizon.

Statement: Set Sail

This photo is at sunset on a beach in Key West. This is the back cover of the Coffee Table book and the message is to think about, use, and move forward with the information in the book. The comment on the last written page of the book without a photo is "You have the power to make the world a better place." The "set sail" is *go do it*.

Chapter 3-3
COFFEE TABLE WRAP-UP

I hope that the review of the Coffee Table book was enjoyable and helpful in providing more examples of real life and relationships to the fundamentals. These topics were triggered by the photographs that I took as well as the emotion and experience I had with them. I am certain that the experience was not the same without the photographs but I hope it was still worthwhile.

Other than the few that I called out, I see the topics as being generally uplifting. There are far more uplifting topics and I have thousands of photographs to express the emotions and message for many more topics. I did not intentionally leave topics out, but the purpose was not to try to cover all aspects of life because that would be impossible. The idea was to show that philosophy does not have to be a complex topic and it can apply to all aspects of life. It was also to inspire thought. Hopefully it triggered your impressions of the photos and the comments, such that you would formulate your own philosophy or see the world in just a slightly different and more hopeful way. I encourage you to take your own photos and add captions. Many people do that today with social media outlets; they just don't think about it as philosophy.

There are philosophers out there that will take a very snobbish approach to philosophy and tout the years that they have spent studying and the degree that they may have; that is all about them and not about you. Everybody has a way that they live their life and that is their philosophy, and the study of how and why they do those things is the study of philosophy.

In the wrap-up of Part 2 of this book I added a topic that was very important and had not yet been addressed. That topic was appreciation. I am going to add another topic in this wrap-up that is also very important; laughter. Laughter and humor are key elements of life. I actually find it surprising that the topic was not included in the Coffee Table book. I certainly have enough photos to trigger that emotion and topic in the book. It may be that I, and maybe others, just don't give it enough thought. I love to laugh and I laugh a lot, so it still is a bit of a mystery why it was not included. Maybe that is all the more reason to give it some time now.

There are so many one-liners and quotes about laughter, which is a good indication of its importance. Laughter obviously can lighten a situation, ease stress, and bring people of varying views together. There is no magic bullet but laughter and music get about as close as you can get for me. There are plenty of studies on the positive physical effects of laughing on the body. In addition to the obvious stress relief, studies at Mayo Clinic show that it "enhances your intake of oxygen-rich air, stimulates your heart, lungs and muscles, and increases the endorphins that are released by your brain." [52] Other studies indicate longer-term effects of an increased immune system and reduced pain. While the physical benefits are fantastic, I don't think that many, if any, of us laugh for the *outcome*.

Part 3: Coffee Table

We can laugh because of a trigger and the ability of our mind to recognize the humor in the trigger. We can laugh at ourselves. We can laugh at jokes. We can laugh at a situation. Some can have an impulse laugh that causes them to laugh when others get hurt or when they are nervous. And sometimes we laugh because it seems there is nothing left to do after a sequence of events is so crazy that laughter becomes a mechanism of coping, and a very effective one at that. We laugh for ourselves but not in a selfish way. We do not laugh for an intended or expected outcome. We are being ourselves when we laugh. I believe it is one of the more natural things that we do. It would be a shame to lose or even reduce that outlet of being ourselves. We need it.

Getting back to the Coffee Table book…when you look around your house, your neighborhood, your family, or the entire world in which we live, you can see opportunities for photographs. These are also opportunities to learn, to formulate knowledge, appreciate what is around you, and to assess the impact of everything on you and your fundamentals. Look at the pictures you have; what emotion or thoughts do they create for you? Most probably trigger memories. Think about what emotion or thoughts were present with that memory. Part 3 was just more examples of real life and the vast world in which we live.

The ISBN for the Coffee Table Philosophy book is 9780985678111

FUNDAMENTALS OF LIFE WRAP-UP

The interaction between your fundamentals becomes the woven fabric of your foundation, which is the basis on which we can live, evolve, and become "better". The way we live out life is much more driven by who we are than what happens to us, even though it very often does not seem that way. Staying above the challenges takes fortitude, commitment, and belief in yourself and your principles. It takes Love, Hope, Believing, and Honor.

What do I know? What do I believe? What are my priorities? What principles do I live by? What should I believe? What should I do? Who should I trust? These questions and many more were addressed in this book. I am hopeful that you can find yourself on a path to answer them for yourself as well as other questions that will arise throughout your life.

I *know* that I don't know everything and that is a fact. I *believe* that I never will; that is probably a fact but it is a future statement so it cannot be a fact. That in itself is evidence of my belief that there is no future fact because if there were, me never knowing *everything* would certainly be one. I also believe that miraculous things happen that were previously unimaginable, so… I believe that everybody has the potential to impact others, and the world, in a positive way whether they intend to or not. Did the truck driver that ran a red light and sent me to the hospital to get checked know that the doctor would find a cancer that would not have otherwise been found? I am here 42 years later to tell this story. Can I explain how more than 30 tons of truck and gravel hit my small van, spun it around 720 degrees across 4 lanes of highway, and I walked away without a scratch? I did not control that. The driver of the truck did not control that.

We can control very little of the outcome and we know little and yet here we are. Our intent and our effort can impact outcomes, not control them. We define who we are, what is important, and the decisions that we make. The effort is worth it even if we only increase the likelihood of a positive outcome by 1%.

I hope that when you see certain words, clichés, nice phrases, and one-liners in the future, they will have more meaning and make you smile because you understand more than you did before.

Happiness, success, wealth, beauty, energy, acceptance, and peace all come from within. Chasing those things will never work. If a person is chasing success, do they ever stop? Success does not make people happy unless it is internal success. Wealth does not make people happy. The only way that we find anything that matters is from within. Our appreciation for what we have is from within. Our happiness comes from within. Our peace comes from within.

Even after all that talk of coming from within, you are not alone. Friends, family, and other people make life worthwhile. You grow inward and you share outward. Enjoy life!

EPILOGUE

If you are reading this I have already claimed success multiple times. I claimed success along the way with writing each chapter, working through the editing process with Deb, designing the cover, formatting the book, getting it printed and setting up the distribution. You reading this book could not be my reasonable goal since I do not have control of that, but it was a desire and I do *appreciate* you reading it, and I greatly appreciate being alive to finish this book.

I have learned a lot while writing this book. As with life, very little of what I have learned are facts but they have increased my knowledge. I will continue to learn for as long as I am able. I am doing the things that I want and need to do. While I have been writing this book, I finished one album and am nearly finished with a second. I am not sure that two albums to one book is significant but it is more information for my future planning.

I was asked about the relationship between my music and my writing. Does one inspire the other? I had a pretty fast answer that they are just different and one is not directly related to the other. I do believe that to be true because they are different formats and different processes. What they do have in common is that they obviously both came from me and who I am. They both express my beliefs, my philosophy, and my observations of life. In that, they are related and consistent.

I have no idea what my next book will be or what my next song will be. And that is a wonderful thing!

Rick Jason

BIBLIOGRAPHY

1. Chapter 1-1, Page 5, Merriam-Webster, merriam-webster.com, https://www.merriam-webster.com/dictionary/fundamental, accessed 11/8/2020
2. Chapter 1-2, Page 12, W. S. Gilbert, 1836 -1911, Iolanthe or "The Peer and the Peri" opera
3. Chapter 1-2, Page 12, Merriam-Webster, wordcentral.com, http://wordcentral.com/cgi-bin/student?love, accessed 11/8/2020
4. Chapter 1-2, Page 14, Merriam-Webster, learnersdictionary.com, https://www.learnersdictionary.com/definition/relationship, accessed 11/8/2020
5. Chapter 1-2, Page 14, Merriam-Webster, learnersdictionary.com, https://www.learnersdictionary.com/definition/relationship, accessed 11/8/2020
6. Chapter 1-3, Page 30, Merriam-Webster, merriam-webster.com, https://www.merriam-webster.com/dictionary/honor, accessed 11/9/2020
7. Chapter 1-3, Page 32, Merriam-Webster, merriam-webster.com, https://www.merriam-webster.com/dictionary/principle, accessed 11/9/2020
8. Chapter 1-4, Page 39, Merriam-Webster, merriam-webster.com, https://www.merriam-webster.com/dictionary/believe, accessed 11/9/2020
9. Chapter 1-4, Page 39, Merriam-Webster, merriam-webster.com, https://www.merriam-webster.com/dictionary/belief, accessed 11/9/2020
10. Chapter 1-5, Page 50, Noah Webster, An American Dictionary of the English Language Vol. 1, Published by S. Converse, 1828

11. Chapter 1-5, Page 51, Some attribute to Albert Einstein, some to Benjamin Franklin, and some to others. Proof of origin is unverified
12. Chapter 1-6, Page 58, Florida State University Philosophy Dept., philosophy.fsu.edu, https://philosophy.fsu.edu/undergraduate-study/why-philosophy/What-is-Philosophy, accessed 11/9/2020
13. Chapter 1-6, Page 64, Aristotle, Aristotle's Metaphysics - Book VIII, (This is frequently misquoted and the translations are varied, the quote in this book may well not be acurate but it is very common). Many Internet sites dispute the translation
14. Chapter 2-3, Page 92, There is no actual evidence to cite Mark Twain even though it is widely believed, others have been named as well, all unproven according to various sources
15. Chapter 2-3, Page 92, Benjamin Franklin, in a letter dated November 13, 1789 which he wrote to the French physicist Jean Baptiste Le Roy, "similar" statements were made prior to this date
16. Chapter 2-6, Page 109, Merriam-Webster, merriam-webster.com, https://www.merriam-webster.com/dictionary/knowledge, accessed 11/9/2020
17. Chapter 2-6, Page 110, This is a widely used phrase, no confirmed origin can be found, however there are a number of speculations (none that I can cite as fact)
18. Chapter 2-7, Page 113, Sophocles (496-406 BC), "Sophocles Quotes." BrainyQuote.com. BrainyMedia Inc, 2020, https://www.brainyquote.com/quotes/sophocles_101515, accessed 11/10/2020
19. Chapter 2-7, Page 113, Socrates (469-399), "Socrates Quotes." BrainyQuote.com. BrainyMedia Inc, 2020, https://www.brainyquote.com/quotes/socrates_391046, accessed 11/10/2020
20. Chapter 2-7, Page 113, Friedrich Nietzsche, Widely accredited to Friedrich Nietzsche however no actual source could be identified
21. Chapter 2-7, Page 113, Confucius, 551-479 BC

22. Chapter 2-7, Page 114, Merriam-Webster, merriam-webster.com, https://www.merriam-webster.com/dictionary/wisdom, accessed 11/10/2020

23. Chapter 2-8. Page119, Merriam-Webster, merriam-webster.com, https://www.merriam-webster.com/dictionary/consistent, accessed 11/24/2020

24. Chapter 2-9, Page 121, Merriam-Webster, merriam-webster.com, https://www.merriam-webster.com/dictionary/integrity, accessed 11/10/2020

25. Chapter 2-9, Page 121, Merriam-Webster, merriam-webster.com, https://www.merriam-webster.com/dictionary/moral, accessed 11/10/2020

26. Chapter 2-9, Page 121, Merriam-Webster, merriam-webster.com, https://www.merriam-webster.com/dictionary/right, accessed 11/11/2020

27. Chapter 2-10, Page 128, Merriam-Webster, merriam-webster.com, https://www.merriam-webster.com/dictionary/trust, accessed 11/11/2020

28. Chapter 2-11, Page 131, Merriam-Webster, learnersdictionary.com, https://learnersdictionary/definition/respect, accessed 12/22/2020

29. Chapter 2-12, Page 137, Merriam-Webster Student Dictionary, wordcentral.com, http://wordcentral.com/cgi-bin/student?book=Student&va=friend, accessed 11/11/2020

30. Chapter 2-12, Page 138, Merriam-Webster, merriam-webster.com, https://www.merriam-webster.com/dictionary/friendship, accessed 11/11/2020

31. Chapter 2-12, Page 139, Aristotle 350 B.C.E., Nicomachean Ethics (Book VIII), Translated by W.D. Ross 1908, Oxford Clarendon Press

32. Chapter 2-14, Page 146, Merriam-Webster, merriam-webster.com, https://www.merriam-webster.com/dictionary/success, accessed 11/12/2020

33. Chapter 2-14, Page 146, Merriam-Webster, merriam-webster.com, https://www.merriam-webster.com/dictionary/succeed, accessed 11/12/2020

34. Chapter 2-15, Page 150, Sir John Dalberg-Acton, Letter to Bishop Mandell Creighton, April 5, 1887 Transcript of, published in Historical Essays and Studies, edited by J. N. Figgis and R. V. Laurence (London: Macmillan, 1907)

35. Chapter 2-15, Page 150, Merriam-Webster, merriam-webster.com, https://www.merriam-webster.com/dictionary/power, accessed 11/12/2020

36. Chapter 2-16, Page 157, Merriam-Webster, merriam-webster.com, https://www.merriam-webster.com/dictionary/deserve, accessed 11/12/2020

37. Chapter 2-17, Page 160, Eliot, George, 1819-1880. The Mill on the Floss. Edinburgh ; London :W. Blackwood and Sons, 1860. (This is not a precise quote but rather an idiom based on the similar statement of the same meaning)

38. Chapter 2-18, Page 165, Merriam-Webster, merriam-webster.com, https://www.merriam-webster.com/dictionary/greed, accessed 11/12/2020

39. Chapter 2-18, Page 166, Merriam-Webster, merriam-webster.com, https://www.merriam-webster.com/dictionary/selfish, accessed 11/12/2020

40. Chapter 2-19, Page 169, William Shakespeare, Hamlet, "William Shakespeare Quotes." Quotes.net. STANDS4 LLC, 2020. Web. 12 Nov. 2020. <https://www.quotes.net/quote/34516>, accessed 11/12/2020

41. Chapter 2-21, Page 176, Franklin D. Roosevelt, Inaugural address, stated during his presidency according to FDR Presidential Library & Museum
42. Chapter 2-21, Page 182, Franklin D. Roosevelt, stated during his presidency according to FDR Presidential Library & Museum
43. Chapter 2-23, Page 187, Merriam-Webster, merriam-webster.com, https://www.merriam-webster.com/dictionary/hate, accessed 11/12/2020
44. Chapter 2-23, Page 187, Merriam-Webster, merriam-webster.com, https://www.merriam-webster.com/dictionary/hate, accessed 11/12/2020
45. Chapter 2-24, Page 191, Benjamin Franklin, in a letter dated November 13, 1789 which he wrote to the French physicist Jean Baptiste Le Roy, "similar" statements were made prior to this date
46. Chapter 2-24, Page 193, Mahatma Gandhi, "Mahatma Gandhi Quotes." BrainyQuote.com. BrainyMedia Inc, 2020, https://www.brainyquote.com/quotes/mahatma_gandhi_133995, accessed 11/12/2020
47. Chapter 2-26, Page 200, Merriam-Webster, merriam-webster.com, https://www.merriam-webster.com/dictionary/pride, accessed 11/11/2020
48. Chapter 2-26, Page 200, Merriam-Webster, merriam-webster.com, https://www.merriam-webster.com/dictionary/self-esteem, accessed 11/11/2020
49. Chapter 2-26, Page 200, Merriam-Webster, merriam-webster.com, https://www.merriam-webster.com/dictionary/self-respect, accessed 11/11/2020
50. Chapter 2-27, Page 206, Heraclitus (c. 500 BC), Greek philosopher
51. Chapter 3-2, Page 258, Franklin D. Roosevelt, Inaugural address, stated during his presidency according to FDR Presidential Library & Museum (note: this is a paraphrased statement from CTP book)

52. Chapter 3-3, Page 282, Mayo Clinic Staff, mayoclinic.org, https://www.mayoclinic.org/healthy-lifestyle/stress-management/in-depth/stress-relief/art-20044456, accessed 11/12/2020

Index

A

age xiii, 91, 111, 134, 135, 142, 162, 185, 211, 215, 246, 261, 264, 266
anxiety 9, 176, 177, 180, 215
appreciation 20, 21, 24, 133, 201, 215, 216, 223, 224, 240, 256, 271, 282, 286

B

beauty 248, 271, 273, 286
belief 10, 39, 40, 41, 42, 43, 44, 45, 46, 49, 50, 51, 58, 59, 60, 61, 62, 63, 114, 123, 177, 178, 205, 216, 231, 232, 254, 259, 260, 285
believe x, xi, 21, 22, 26, 31, 32, 33, 39, 40, 41, 42, 43, 44, 45, 46, 50, 51, 53, 55, 58, 59, 61, 62, 63, 64, 75, 85, 87, 88, 90, 92, 93, 94, 95, 103, 105, 106, 109, 110, 115, 117, 119, 122, 125, 126, 127, 128, 132, 135, 142, 152, 155, 156, 157, 159, 162, 169, 178, 179, 188, 191, 194, 202, 204, 205, 207, 210, 217, 218, 220, 222, 223, 231, 234, 238, 239, 246, 250, 252, 254, 259, 260, 261, 270, 273, 275, 277, 283, 285, 286, A-i
believing 22, 32, 36, 39, 40, 41, 43, 46, 47, 50, 51, 53, 54, 59, 63, 64, 123, 191, 200, 202, 207, 234, 235, 253

C

change xi, 7, 17, 18, 41, 42, 45, 46, 70, 86, 92, 93, 106, 122, 135, 147, 178, 184, 194, 196, 206, 212, 215, 216, 237, 238, 240, 246, 248, 256, 259, 260, 261, 263, 264, 266, 269, 276
circle 20, 51, 57, 70, 71, 73, 74, 75, 82, 91, 97, 107, 114, 115, 140, 143, 150, 176, 178, 181, 219, 220
common denominator 6, 7, 217, 223, 255
consistency 18, 29, 33, 36, 49, 70, 76, 123, 124, 169, 192, 201, 206, 232
consistent 13, 31, 33, 35, 36, 63, 71, 74, 119, 121, 122, 134, 186, 188, 206, 220, A-i
context xiv, 17, 24, 25, 26, 27, 45, 46, 52, 54, 60, 61, 66, 67, 69, 74, 86, 87, 88, 89, 90, 92, 93, 94, 100, 102, 106, 109, 110, 111, 119, 125, 126, 127, 128, 132, 150, 160, 166, 183, 184, 189, 193, 195, 196, 201, 209, 210, 211, 216, 221, 223, 231, 232, 235, 239, 241, 247, 248, 254, 256, 277
control 4, 21, 22, 25, 54, 60, 67, 68, 71, 83, 117, 143, 144, 146, 147, 148, 149, 150, 151, 152, 153, 156, 157, 159, 162, 170, 177, 178, 179, 180, 188, 221, 222, 228, 230, 242, 243, 252, 254, 262, 270, 273, 286, A-i
cross-check 8, 72
crossroads 205, 206

D

decisions xi, 3, 5, 6, 8, 9, 10, 12, 13, 17, 19, 20, 21, 24, 25, 26, 27, 34, 35, 37, 45, 46, 49, 51, 52, 53, 57, 59, 61, 63, 65, 66, 67, 68, 69, 72, 75, 76, 77, 81, 83, 91, 94, 96, 97, 105, 119, 123, 126, 127, 128, 129, 133, 136, 141, 142, 146, 151, 153, 157, 160, 169, 176, 177, 179, 184, 185, 186, 188, 192, 194, 195, 196, 201, 205, 206, 207, 209, 212, 217, 219, 223, 230, 247, 253, 276, 286

E

elderly ix, 134, 135, 264, 266
emotions 13, 22, 44, 60, 66, 92, 118, 176, 209, 210, 241, 272, 281
expectation xiv, 19, 44, 50, 51, 125, 155, 156, 160, 197, 216, 228, 260
external influencers 66, 74, 81, 91, 151, 181, 186, 222, 223

F

fabric 10, 26, 27, 29, 32, 34, 35, 37, 46, 55, 57, 60, 61, 64, 65, 67, 69, 181, 196, 218, 263, 285
fact x, xi, xiii, xiv, 8, 15, 16, 20, 23, 32, 39, 40, 41, 42, 43, 45, 46, 49, 51, 53, 58, 61, 64, 67, 87, 88, 90, 94, 96, 100, 103, 104, 105, 106, 107, 109, 111, 116, 122, 127, 134, 150, 151, 155, 160, 169, 170, 192, 197, 203, 207, 209, 210, 215, 216, 217, 222, 228, 230, 234, 237, 239, 249, 250, 251, 255, 256, 262, 266, 285, 286
faith 39, 41, 43, 45, 46, 63, 191, 235, 245, 250, 251, 260
family x, xi, 11, 16, 17, 54, 160, 191, 192, 195, 196, 218, 242, 266, 283, 286
fear xiv, 8, 9, 15, 67, 175, 176, 177, 178, 179, 180, 181, 182, 187, 191, 235, 245, 258, 259, 262
freedom 151, 204, 246, 252, 253, 254, 270, 274
friend 12, 16, 21, 42, 68, 96, 137, 138, 139, 193, 211, 236
future 25, 43, 52, 104, 111, 155, 192, 196, 207, 211, 235, 275, 276, 285, 286, A-i

G

goal 31, 52, 54, 55, 63, 145, 146, 147, 202, 211, 216, 218, 228, A-i
goals 52, 67, 76, 146, 147, 148, 218, 230
God 17, 19, 23, 39, 41, 43, 62, 63, 216, 251
greed 162, 165, 166, 230, 261
grounding 6, 29, 46, 222, 244, 260, 261, 262
guidelines 7, 9, 59, 146, 170, 178, 197, 223, 239

H

honor 22, 29, 30, 31, 32, 33, 34, 36, 37, 40, 49, 55, 63, 113, 116, 119, 121, 122, 129, 132, 134, 168, 197, 199, 222, 230, 231, 234, 253
hope xiii, xiv, 22, 33, 49, 50, 51, 52, 53, 54, 55, 63, 64, 123, 126, 128, 134, 146, 148, 157, 158, 168, 177, 178, 189, 194, 199, 211, 220, 221, 222, 230, 231, 234, 237, 240, 241, 245, 250, 251, 253, 258, 260, 278, 281, 227
humanity 11, 14, 18, 21, 23, 63, 76, 110, 114

I

impact x, xi, 3, 4, 5, 10, 17, 18, 21, 24, 25, 26, 34, 35, 45, 53, 61, 66, 67, 69, 71, 74, 81, 82, 86, 87, 92, 102, 103, 107, 110, 128, 139, 141, 146, 147, 156, 178, 180, 181, 184, 185, 186, 189, 192, 195, 198, 200, 201, 205, 210, 219, 221, 232, 242, 243, 244, 245, 247, 252, 254, 256, 261, 266, 275, 277, 278, 283, 286
inner core 72, 73, 74, 81, 95, 107, 115, 141, 181, 197, 198, 221, 224, 246, 263, 267, 273, 275, 278
inner peace 6, 9, 27, 34, 37, 57, 61, 63, 70, 112, 119, 143, 169, 173, 181, 197, 204, 217, 224, 245, 259, 278
integrity 29, 30, 49, 83, 100, 101, 116, 121, 122, 123, 124, 127, 128, 158, 167, 195, 201, 212

K

knowledge 35, 58, 66, 70, 71, 72, 73, 74, 91, 92, 95, 96, 97, 105, 107, 109, 110, 111, 112, 114, 116, 126, 129, 134, 151, 153, 158, 181, 183, 197, 212, 230, 237, 238, 240, 246, 257, 262, 264, 267, 276, 283, A-i

L

laughter 282, 283
light 119, 201, 237, 245, 246, 286
listen 45, 92, 94, 97, 100, 101, 127, 136, 240, 246, 247
love xi, 8, 11, 12, 13, 14, 15, 16, 17, 18, 19, 20, 21, 22, 23, 24, 25, 26, 29, 33, 49, 55, 61, 63, 64, 66, 69, 116, 126, 132, 133, 137, 139, 140, 187, 188, 193, 199, 222, 231, 234, 236, 240, 253, 258, 265, 268, 269, 272, 277, 278, 282

M

music ix, xi, 5, 20, 172, 232, 240, 241, 243, 244, 282, A-i

N

negative influences 66, 81, 221
noise 3, 9, 10, 67, 68, 69, 70, 72, 95, 97, 195, 197, 257

O

old 89, 97, 134, 135, 185, 215, 223, 238, 265, 266
outcome 20, 22, 51, 52, 53, 59, 99, 117, 146, 148, 149, 153, 156, 157, 163, 170, 206, 207, 230, 243, 259, 282, 283, 286

P

pain 67, 90, 183, 184, 185, 186, 282
pattern 20, 69, 96, 98, 212, 276
perception 41, 42, 43, 44, 46, 50, 51, 70, 76, 86, 88, 101, 103, 104, 105, 106, 111, 122, 142, 145, 151, 158, 170, 177, 181, 185, 199, 201, 202, 222, 230, 237, 238, 245, 246, 247, 248, 249, 250, 251, 255, 260, 264, 266

Philosophies
  Altruism 61
  Buddhism 62
  Determinism 59
  Hedonism 59, 166
  Nihilism 59
  Relationalism 60
  Relativism 60, 85, 90
  Stoicism 60
  Taoism 61
prejudice 42, 159, 161, 162
principles 10, 18, 20, 32, 33, 35, 36, 40, 41, 45, 46, 49, 54, 59, 63, 66, 67, 68, 69, 70, 71, 83, 95, 100, 115, 116, 117, 118, 119, 121, 122, 123, 124, 128, 129, 132, 140, 147, 148, 151, 153, 162, 166, 172, 177, 178, 183, 186, 189, 195, 197, 198, 207, 222, 223, 230, 239, 243, 247, 248, 254, 259, 285
priorities xi, 6, 17, 18, 61, 66, 69, 70, 116, 118, 123, 124, 126, 128, 184, 192, 194, 195, 196, 197, 205, 221, 222, 257, 273, 277, 285
process xi, xiv, 7, 11, 24, 29, 31, 33, 40, 57, 62, 68, 70, 72, 74, 75, 82, 86, 88, 89, 91, 94, 114, 119, 123, 160, 169, 181, 197, 212, 223, 239, 241, 276, A-i

R

relative ix, 9, 12, 14, 16, 60, 85, 86, 88, 90, 99, 101, 105, 184, 221, 237, 241, 248, 259, 260, 272
respect 4, 6, 19, 20, 23, 29, 30, 31, 34, 35, 37, 83, 94, 105, 116, 125, 128, 131, 132, 133, 134, 135, 136, 140, 148, 150, 158, 173, 197, 199, 200, 201, 203, 216, 229, 230, 231, 246, 247, 253, 255, 263, 264, 265, 267, 269, 274
responsibility 12, 59, 71, 99, 107, 117, 125, 127, 133, 134, 151, 152, 158, 167, 168, 169, 170, 178, 189, 200, 224, 229, 230, 227, 234
right and wrong 21, 36, 45, 70, 121, 123, 222, 262

S

satisfaction x, 70, 168, 192, 200, 215
self-esteem 4, 19, 20, 34, 143, 148, 181, 197, 199, 200, 201, 202, 216, 230
self-respect 4, 20, 23, 34, 35, 37, 148, 150, 173, 197, 199, 200, 201, 203, 216, 230, 247
self-things 199, 202, 204, 216, 223, 252, 275, 278
social media 17, 42, 102, 139, 230, 282
subjective 9, 31, 53, 67, 105, 183, 238
success 67, 145, 146, 147, 148, 150, 166, 199, 201, 228, 230, 242, 286, A-i

T

traumas xi, 8
true 4, 17, 19, 31, 33, 34, 35, 36, 39, 40, 45, 53, 59, 63, 64, 76, 92, 93, 104, 122, 124, 136, 139, 148, 168, 169, 170, 183, 185, 189, 193, 203, 204, 206, 219, 222, 223, 230, 237, 250, 258, 265, 268, 277, A-i
trust 16, 22, 29, 34, 35, 39, 40, 42, 89, 105, 106, 107, 116, 125, 126, 128, 129, 133, 135,

136, 137, 138, 139, 140, 151, 152, 155, 156, 158, 169, 200, 201, 229, 230, 245, 262, 273, 274, 285
truth 12, 41, 44, 60, 76, 85, 89, 103, 122, 128, 230, 237, 238, 248, 249, 250, 251, 264
tuning 7, 11, 25, 60, 70, 71, 72, 75, 82, 91, 112, 128, 192, 219, 223, 248

V

validation 7, 8, 27, 33, 40, 44, 68, 76, 77, 116, 119, 122, 172, 230
values 31, 32, 36, 87, 121, 238, 256, 260, 264, 273

W

why x, xi, 5, 6, 11, 17, 20, 31, 65, 69, 75, 82, 95, 97, 104, 105, 106, 113, 114, 115, 116, 118, 123, 133, 134, 135, 143, 166, 172, 181, 184, 191, 202, 205, 206, 215, 217, 218, 220, 222, 223, 228, 239, 241, 242, 247, 250, 251, 255, 258, 260, 261, 264, 278, 282
worry 175, 176, 178, 181, 247, 258

Y

yourself 4, 10, 12, 14, 16, 17, 18, 19, 20, 23, 24, 25, 26, 34, 35, 46, 57, 63, 68, 70, 71, 74, 76, 77, 86, 98, 101, 102, 111, 122, 123, 124, 125, 126, 129, 134, 136, 142, 143, 146, 148, 152, 153, 167, 169, 170, 177, 178, 186, 188, 189, 201, 202, 204, 210, 218, 219, 223, 224, 235, 244, 246, 247, 258, 259, 260, 261, 262, 268, 273, 277, 285

www.ingramcontent.com/pod-product-compliance
Lightning Source LLC
Chambersburg PA
CBHW071856290426
44110CB00013B/1175